A TREASURY OF TEXAS HUMOR

BILL CANNON

REPUBLIC OF TEXAS PRESS

Dallas • Lanham • Boulder • New York • Toronto • Plymouth, UK

Published by Republic of Texas Press
An imprint of The Rowman & Littlefield Publishing Group, Inc.
4501 Forbes Boulevard, Suite 200
Lanham, MD 20706
http://www.rlpgtrade.com

10 Thornbury Road, Plymouth PL6 7PP, United Kingdom

Distributed by NATIONAL BOOK NETWORK

Library of Congress Cataloging-in-Publication Data available

Cannon, Bill.
 A treasury of Texas humor / Bill Cannon.
  p. cm.
 ISBN 13: 978-1-55622-693-4

 1. American wit and wisdom—Texas. 2. Texas—Humor.

PN6231.T56 C36   2001
                                        99-049385
817.008'032764—dc21   CIP

⊖™ The paper used in this publication meets the minimum requirements of American National Standard for Information Sciences—Permanence of Paper for Printed Library Materials, ANSI/NISO Z39.48-1992.

Manufactured in the United States of America.

DEDICATION

This book is dedicated to my father, Eugene Cannon, whose sense of humor, second only to his faith in God, got him over life's rough spots.

CONTENTS

INTRODUCTION

TEXAS HUMOR LURKS BEHIND EVERY PRICKLY PEAR

A distinct part of this state that we call Texas is its humor. Humor lurks behind every prickly pear in Texas. Humor can be sifted from its history, its multicultural inhabitants, its politics, and its geographical settings, such as the naming of its communities and cities. Some of its shortcomings are made palatable through its humor. A graphic example is found in its reputation for bragging. Texans are expected to brag that everything is bigger, grander, and more desirable than anywhere else on the planet. Its point of departure for its bragging has always been its size.

The vastness of the state made it possible, since its annexation into the United States, to brag that "Texas, with its 267,277 square miles, was the largest state in the Union." That was until 1959, when Alaska with its 656,424 square miles became the nation's 49th state. Then Texas was forced to change its tune. For a Texan this was not easy to swallow! Instead of pouting like a kid who had lost his place in line at the movies, Texans reverted to their built-in humor and without missing a step proudly announced that "Texas was the largest unfrozen state in the Union!"

Adversity has a way of stimulating Texans. They use it to aggrandize Texas by falling back on their humor to

take out the sting. One example of a Texan's use of
adversity to brag about the state's "firstness" in all
aspects of life, also points out the Texan's fervent belief
that only by the divine favor of a Supreme Being could
our state have risen to such lofty heights. It is the story
of a West Texas cowboy who, while lost in the Big Bend
region of the state, wandered into a small graveyard in a
Brewster County community. The story goes that the
cowpoke fell into a freshly dug grave, which awaited a
scheduled funeral. Although perplexed at his dilemma,
the wayward cowhand decided to sleep away the night
and take a fresh look at things by the light of a new day.
The following morning the sun came up over the Chisos
Mountains in a burst of light and color that only a West
Texas sunrise can afford. Having slept soundly the
entire night, the cowpoke was not immediately aware of
his circumstances, except for the fact that he was in a
deep hole. He managed to pull and claw himself to
ground level, where he looked around and saw the grave
markers. He then realized he was in a cemetery. He was
blinded by the brilliancy of the sunrise. In true Texas
spirit, he shouted to a nonexistent audience, "Texas,
first in the resurrection!"

ON TEXAS TALL TALES

Tall tales are stories, generally told in jest, that are so obviously exaggerated so as to be unbelievable, as most of them are. Notice we said "most" tall tales are accredited to, or expected of, Texans, no doubt, because of the stories told around the campfires by bored and lonesome cowboys. Perhaps the origin of Texas tall tales and "Daddy" of them all were those told about the mythical Texas cowboy. "Pecos Bill." This West Texas cowpoke, it was said, being an orphan, was raised by a coyote. "Bill" was said to have dug the Grand Canyon with a stick and ridden everything from a mountain lion to a cyclone! As the reputation for pomposity among Texans spread, so did the expectation of their having another exaggerated story out of Texas to tell. And one cannot disappoint a willing listener.

So, like an avid fisherman's unlikely fish stories, Texans milked their reputations for all it was worth. Our offerings here consist of only a handful of the more mild Texas tales. But, one has to be careful before judging them to be a lie. Knowing Texas, they just might be true!

A LESSON ON THOROUGHNESS

In recent years those who attend or have attended the very respected Texas A&M University have been the butt of many jokes pointed at their learned intelligence. Perhaps the origin of these generally untrue stories was an incident that occurred a decade or so ago. A newspaper story of that time related that a two-seated Cessna airplane had crashed in a cemetery not far from College Station. The university had generously sent a search and rescue team of volunteers from the school and at last report, they had recovered 300 bodies and were still digging!

THE NAKED TRUTH ABOUT TEXANS' WEALTH

Two Texans made a trip to a newly opened Louisiana casino. They agreed to meet early the next morning at the casino lounge. Both, not wanting to miss a thing, came down immediately upon getting out of bed. Arriving at the lounge, one Texan, still in his underwear, was met by his friend who was totally naked. The naked Texan

said to his friend in his underwear, "I really envy you—
you always know when to quit!"

A BAD COFFIN SPELL

There are many folks, particularly those from outside our state, who have the opinion that Texas is one
flat prairie. Perhaps this story will convince them that
we have some pretty steep hills also. The story was told
at a Central Texas Lion's Club luncheon.

It is said that one beautiful little Texas town, which
is the county seat of a Hill Country county, sits at the
foot of one of the state's longest hills on an interstate
highway. The hill has such a steep grade that one stay-
ing in nearby motels can hear the big eighteen-wheelers
grind their gears trying to come into town at a safe
speed! At the top of this hill, and a few hundred feet off
the interstate, in a small stand of trees is the Mt. Pisgah
Missionary Baptist Church. One of its longtime

members, Sister Ludi Mae Simpson, had died and her funeral was planned at the church with burial in the small town.

After the last three verses of "Rock of Ages" were sung, Sister Simpson's coffin was loaded in the back of a hearse to be driven to the cemetery. The hearse had to cross a small bar ditch between the churchyard and the highway. The sudden jolt caused by crossing the ditch resulted in the rear doors of the hearse coming unlocked.

After pulling out on the interstate, the vehicle lurched into motion. The movement sent the coffin bearing Mrs. Simpson out of the hearse where it landed flat on the pavement and squarely on the white line in the middle of the interstate, as if directed there by the Almighty, Himself! The steep slope of the hill was such that the coffin started sliding down the interstate in the direction of the county seat about half a mile below. As the coffin continued downhill it began to pick up speed, slowly at first and then faster and faster until it reached a speed of 75 to 80 miles per hour.

At this speed it didn't take long for Mrs. Ludi Mae to reach the city limits! The pine coffin was smoking slightly by the time it ran through the town's only sig-nal light, which hung from poles at the intersection by the town square. Fortunately for the speeding corpse, the light was green when she flashed through at a speed quite a bit above the speed limit! The coffin whizzed by the Confederate statue on the courthouse lawn. Fortu-nately, by this time the coffin had lost most of its speed. It crossed the street around the square doing only about 30 mph, when it jumped the curb and hit the double doors of Rexal Drugs. It crashed through the doors, flew

4

past the front register, past the candy display, and flew past the cosmetic counter.

It came to an abrupt stop when it hit the prescription counter. The sudden stop caused the coffin lid to fly off and Ludi Mae, who was known to all, to sit straight up in the now immobile coffin. Wilburn Moody, who had been the druggist at the store for nearly twenty years, said the same thing he had said daily since he started working there, "May I help you?"

To this Mrs. Simpson gave a perfectly legitimate reply, "Can you please give me something to stop this coffin?"

I can't vouch for the truthfulness of this story, but it impressed Ace Pollard enough that he gave the teller a job selling previously owned cars at the Chevrolet house.

"BIG JOHN" COMES TO PECOS!

In all his days behind the bar at the Golden Nugget Saloon in Pecos, Sam the bartender had never received instructions from the saloon's owner like he got this evening. "Big John" is going to be in town, I hear. If he comes in, I want you to close the bar, take the cash box to the office, and lock the place up! Just drop everything and run for your life if you hear that "Big John" is coming to town!

About nine o'clock, a man came running into the Nugget. "Big John is coming!" he shouted for all to hear. About that time, the swinging doors were about knocked off their hinges. Pushing his way through a few trail bums standing in the doorway, in strode a giant of a man over six foot tall and sporting a bushy red beard that covered his neck and much of his chest. Card players flew in all directions as the man, without comment, overturned the first two tables that stood between him and the bar. The oak bar was nearly split in half when he pounded his ham-sized fists to get the bartender's attention. "Bottle of whiskey," he said in a demanding voice that overshadowed the piano music that previously had filled the room. The bartender meekly slid a bottle of two-dollar red-eye the length of the bar into the grip of the hulk of a man that awaited it. All eyes were fastened on the man with the bushy beard as he bit off the top of the bottle with his teeth and spat it into the polished spittoon that sat at his feet! He consumed the bottle almost without removing it from his now moist lips.

"Want another?" asked the bartender meekly. "Naw!" replied the burly customer, "I ain't going to hang around long. Don't want to be here if Big John comes in!"

THE BORROWED QUOTATION

A Dallas historian and photographer was told that each year on the anniversary of his fatal shooting, the ghost of Texas badman Sam Bass appeared in the lobby of the Round Rock Bank, where he was mortally wounded attempting to rob the bank. "What a scoop it would be if I could capture the infamous man's ghost on film," he thought. On the appropriate day the following July, the historian meticulously set up his camera in the bank's lobby and quietly awaited the ghost's appearance. True to what he had been told, about noon Bass' ghost showed itself. The photographer popped in a flash bulb and snapped the shutter. When the film was developed he was disappointed to find that the negative was terribly underexposed. It was almost blank! In a moment of quiet desperation the man said aloud, *"The spirit was willing, but the flash was weak!"*

EVEN TEXAS ROAD KILL
CAN BE HUMOROUS

Normally, road kill doesn't deserve special attention; however, if you live in Texas, it may serve to verify a Texan's reputation to exaggerate. My friend, Ray Sims tells of an East Texas buddy of his who has a rural home that sits on a main highway near Henderson. Ray related how his friend, who's veracity is, or was, before this story, beyond doubt. He told Ray about an experience he had one sleepy weekend as he sat on his front porch watching the pickups drive by. He related how one of those Texas "good-ol-boys" abruptly stopped his pickup near his house. The driver jumped out of his truck and walked to a spot in the road, which could be seen by Ray's friend. He then reached in the bed of his truck and produced an aerosol can. The driver returned to the front of his truck, where he bent over the spot in the road and proceeded to spray the spot with the contents of the can.

Ray's friend was more than a little bit curious about the driver's interest in what was obviously the remains of some poor critter that had met the same fate as many other small animals crossing the highway in traffic. Ray's friend told how he saw the driver toss the can into a ditch that ran alongside the road when he was finished with the task. After he drove away, he watched as slowly, almost as if in slow motion, the spot began to show signs of life. First he could see one long ear rise from the pavement. Then another long ear followed.

8

As if in a dream, Ray's friend watched as the spot slowly rose up from the asphalt, made two or three hops, and then started off across the pasture in front of his rural home. The East Texas friend watched in disbelief as the "dead" rabbit bounded across the pasture. It ran about a hundred yards and then turned and waved. The resurrected rabbit ran another few yards and then turned and waved again. This procedure of running, then turning to wave continued until it was out of sight. Still in shock, stated Ray's friend, he couldn't contain himself any longer! He rushed out to the bar ditch to have a look at the discarded can. He picked it up and looked at the label. The miracle-working can was marked *"Hare Restorer with Permanent Wave."*

"JUST BLOW OUT THAT DARNED LANTERN!"

Fish stories know no state boundaries to be suspect, but Texas fish stories are, like everything else, just bigger lies than most! My friend, Ray Sims, who is an avid hunter and fisherman, has probably heard and told more than the average Texas fish stories. One of his buddies down in Austin told Ray how he caught a twenty-pound bass at Toledo Bend Lake. Ray has fished that lake as much as anyone and questioned the man's honesty about his fish.

Ray said, "Let me tell you about the time Pete and I went crappie fishing on Lake Houston. We were fishing at night from the bank and we caught about thirty crappie as fast as we could stick the minners on the hooks."

"That's a whole lot of crappie, ain't it Ray?" asked his doubting buddy.

"That isn't the half of it," said Ray. "Pete got so excited he kicked the lantern in the lake. We went back the next weekend to the same spot to see if we could repeat our luck. I threw out my crappie rig, and when I pulled it in I had hooked our lantern. "And," said Ray, "it was still burning."

"Now," said Ray's friend, "that is about the biggest fish lie I've ever heard."

"Okay," said Ray, "you take ten pounds off your bass, and I'll blow out my lantern!"

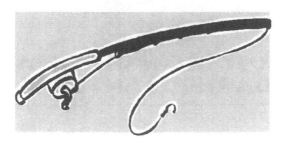

WHAT'S IN A NAME?

One Mills County rancher reported that one local cowpoke was called a rustler, even though he never stole livestock. He got hung with the title because he wore taffeta underwear!

WHY MEDICAL INSURANCE IS COSTLY

In the ritzy Highland Park section of Dallas, the residents demand the ultimate in everything. This does not exclude the medical profession. One young doctor, just opening his practice and having grown up in this environment, opened his office with an expensive but expected flare. His extravagantly appointed office was staffed with a receptionist, two nurses and two assistant nurses, one lab technician, and himself. Service was to be paramount in his office!

One day a man about thirty years of age strolled in. "What can we do for you?" asked the receptionist.

"I have the shingles," replied the young man.

"Have a seat over there and fill out these patient information forms," she instructed. After about thirty

minutes, the receptionist picked up the forms and ush-
ered the man into a waiting room. After a wait of thirty
or so minutes, a lady in white, who introduced herself as
an assistant nurse entered the room and asked what the
man needed.

"As I told the lady at the desk, I have the shingles."
The assistant nurse escorted the man straight to an
examination room.

"You may hang your jacket on that hook," she said.
She then stepped out and returned with the nurse. The
nurse proceeded to tell the impatient man to remove all
his clothes and lay down on the examination table. The
man lay quietly for about a half hour.

The silence was broken by the entrance of a man in
a lab coat who introduced himself as the technician.
"I'm here to draw blood and do an EKG," said the man.
"When I am finished, the doctor will examine you." The
procedures took about thirty minutes. As promised, the
doctor then made his appearance. "And, young man," he
said, "I understand you have the shingles?" To which
the now exasperated man replied, "Yes I do!"

"Let me have a look," said the doctor as he started
examining the man. After looking over the man's nude
body, he said, "turn over." The young man complied.
"And," asked the doctor after his examination, "Just
where are the shingles?"

"They are on my truck," said the deliveryman, "they
are the ones you ordered from the lumber yard!"

As the frustrated doctor left, followed by the equally
frustrated man, the nurse handed the man a sizable bill.

100 PROOF MOSQUITO STORY

Weekend fishing trips for Texans are quite common, providing their teams are not playing on TV on the weekend selected for the outing. These fishing trips are fraught with a variety of risks, one of the most common of which is the ever-present, always hungry, mosquitoes. If one sleeps out at night, he must come prepared to fend off the buzzing, needle-nosed, curse of the outdoorsman! While sitting around a campfire at the end of a hard day's fishing on the Colorado River, three men were discussing their escape from the cares of life with a three-day fishing trip. One man, in discussing a third man, remarked that he didn't understand how he could sleep at night without a mosquito net.

The second fisherman said, "Easy to explain, the first half of the night he is so drunk that when the mosquitoes stick him he doesn't bleed. The second half of the night, the mosquitoes are too drunk to stick him anymore!"

TEXAS ISN'T THE ONLY PLACE WITH BAD TIMES IN THE "OIL PATCH"!

A Texas oil billionaire was in Paris on a vacation. As he stood gazing at the Eiffel Tower he turned to a man standing beside him and said, "I've been coming here for ten years and they still haven't struck oil!"

TEXAS TALL TALES THAT JUST MIGHT BE TRUE!

OR

THE FIRST LIAR HASN'T GOT A CHANCE!

My father, Eugene Cannon, by material standards, was a poor man. But he left me a legacy that extends beyond material wealth! He had a boundless love for

Texas and was endowed with an ingrained sense of humor, which he freely used to bring smiles and belly laughs to those who were fortunate to be included in his circle of friends. This well-spread wealth of laughter was a testimony to his zest for life! I am grateful that he passed both these traits on to me. His, like most Texans, had the kind of sense of humor that helped see him through the difficult times while growing up in the latter part of the 1800s on a San Saba County farm. Many of his tongue-in-cheek Texas tales were drawn, I am sure, from life experiences. These tales, even if not true, were true to life. They are good examples of how Texans look at themselves and their state.

One story I remember best is a typical lampoon of Texas' much discussed weather. It was told that one summer it got so hot in San Saba County that all the popcorn popped in the fields. This rural calamity was further magnified, my father said, when the family's mule, knowing how fickle Texas weather can be, thought a sudden blizzard had brought a snowstorm and froze to death!

I find that easier to believe than a story he told about a fishing trip he and my Uncle Newt took on Little River near Temple, Texas. These fishermen were ambushed by Texas-size mosquitoes. As if the pesky insects weren't bad enough, those bred in the backwaters of Texas are destined for immortality through the tall tales of Texans like my father.

Sleeping out during a sporting trip would normally be a pleasurable part of the trip, were it not for the gargantuan mosquitoes. My father related how, on their first night under the stars, he and Newt were just dozing off when they were attacked by a swarm of the huge

15

needle-nosed insects. They assembled overhead, he related, like a squadron of dive-bombers. Anticipating the painful attack of the giant mosquitoes' lance-like noses, my father peeked out from under his blanket and located the cast-iron wash pot, which was to serve as a cauldron for frying their catch. He edged his way along the ground until he was close enough to pull the heavy utensil over him, covering him completely.

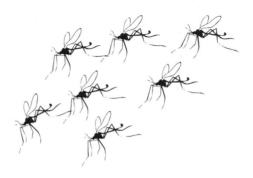

But, he said, the Texas-size mosquitoes were not to be denied! He heard them buzz into formation in the night air directly above him and the cast-iron pot that now covered him. Then came the dreaded scream of their dive straight down in formation, toward the warm human blood they sensed below the dome-like cover. "Could these blood suckers not be outwitted," he thought. Thud!, thud!, thud!, they hit the cast-iron pot one by one. Then, and only then, could their size be truly appreciated.

A quick inspection revealed that they had driven their giant needle-like noses through the cast-iron pot in a quest for the flesh below. My father, who had become a carpenter after leaving the farm, remembered the claw hammer that hung by his side in his ever-present stripped overalls. He silently drew the hammer from its holder. In a swift succession of blows he used the hammer to bend over the ten-penny-size noses of the mosquitoes. He had finally put an end to their attack! He had won the battle of the Texas mosquitoes, or had he?

The whirring of wings overhead signaled a costly and unexpected turn of events. The river bottom mosquitoes, angered, no doubt, by being denied an evening meal, flew away with the valuable cast-iron pot firmly attached to their permanently disfigured noses!

SOMEWHERE BETWEEN TALL TALES AND THE GOD-AWFUL TRUTH!

Recently in Lubbock, I was told that my exaggerated accounts of West Texas' less-than-perfect climate was not just a humorous fabrication but was, indeed, appropriate! They said that any person who had lived west of Fort Worth for at least two seasons could provide their experiences which, at first blush, seemed to be typical Texas tall tales but were, instead, truth! As examples, he offered the following:

"It is so hot in the summer in West Texas that red ants carry little twigs that they stick into the ground and climb up, just to keep their feet off the hot sand.

"Rain is so rare in West Texas the weatherman may report that the area had a "shotgun rainstorm." He explained that a "shotgun rainstorm" was when a farmer stood his double-barreled shotgun against his fence during a rainstorm, and it only rained down one barrel.

On the other hand, those who live in Houston live by the motto, "When it rains it pours!" Some folks in Houston have been known to intentionally inflate the airbags in their cars to be used as floatation devices! My daughter, Cindy, who lives in "Big H," said that one day a fellow worker came back from lunch and said, "Its raining cats and dogs, and I just stepped in a poodle!"

MIGHTY HEAVY GUAGE WIRE, HARRY!

Harry Oglesby down in Mills County was overheard telling someone that the summer heat was so stifling he had to take down the barbed-wire fence around his place just to get a breeze.

ON BRAGGING

Some non-Texans feel that the words Texan and bragging are synonymous. And, perhaps some of our zealots' love and admiration for Texas is manifested by their propounding, what may seem to some as in excess, the many attractive features offered by Texas. While they may be called "braggadocios" by non-Texans, we hasten to point out that boasting is not bragging if its true, which it generally is when talking about Texas!

Regardless, some zealousness is carried far enough that it takes on a humorous tone. As evidence, we present the following stories:

TEXAS BRAGGING BACKFIRES

A Midland man, who was blessed with an oil well, prided himself in always getting the best of everything now that he was wealthy! But he was deaf as a post! His friends encouraged him to get a hearing aid. One day he showed up at his usual hangout, the domino parlor. His friends noticed that his hearing seemed to have improved. "You seem to be hearing much better, Mr. Scott," remarked one player.

"Yes," he replied, hoping someone would notice. "I bought a hearing aid." He couldn't resist bragging about his wealth. "It cost $5,000."

"Five thousand dollars?" responded the player in disbelief. "It must be a fine one, what kind is it?"

The rich old man looked at his wrist and replied, "twelve-thirty!"

BIG BILL SMITH FROM EL PASO

One of the not-so-flattering traits attributed to all
Texans is their alleged pomposity. Most of us
native-born Texans know this is an unwarranted tag
attached to us because of a few inflated egos wandering
around in cowboy hats. This preconceived opinion lends
itself to be caricatured, even by fellow Texans. Such
characterization is typified by the favorite Texas story of
my friend Ray Sims. The story is about a West Texan
who went by the name of "Big Bill Smith of El Paso."

"Big Bill" had the reputation of bragging that he
knew everybody in the world. Not just most of the people, but everybody! This boast came most frequently
after Big Bill had a few bourbons and branch waters
under his gaudy silver belt buckle. Bill was, what we
Texans call, "All hat and no cattle!" When tanked up,
Big Bill started his "I know everybody in the world"
routine.

One evening, on just such an occasion, he was finally
stopped in midsentence by a well-heeled oilman who had
the nerve to contradict Big Bill's boasting, backed up, as
well-heeled Texans are expected to do, by putting his
money on the line. "I'll bet you $500 you don't know
President Lyndon Johnson," who was president at the
time. With this, Big Bill picked up the phone and
instructed the operator to get the White House on the
line. He then asked to speak to Lyndon Johnson, "Tell
him Big Bill Smith from El Paso is calling."

After a brief pause, the warm, soft Texas drawl of
Lyndon Johnson could be heard thanking Big Bill for his

generous campaign contribution. The president also said, "Bird and I want you and the Mrs. to come see us real soon now, ya'll heah?" Those listening were amazed at the confirmation of Big Bill's boast.

His friend paid his wager. Still not satisfied, the oilman bet Big Bill that he didn't know Clint Eastwood. Bill then returned to the speakerphone and dialed a few numbers and started a friendly conversation with the movie star.

The oilman was determined once and for all to let the air out of Big Bill's pomposity. He threw down his final gauntlet, "I'll concede you know a lot of Americans, but the world is a big place. I'll bet you $10,000 you don't know the pope!"

With this Big Bill accepted the challenge, indicating that he and the pontiff were on very good terms. His challenger refused to accept a phone call as proof of Big Bill's relationship with the pontiff.

He told the pompous oilman that they would use his jet to fly to Rome tomorrow to see the pope in person. He then instructed his secretary to have his Lear jet ready for a trip to Rome. The next day found Big Bill and his challenger mingling with about 10,000 people on the square in front of the Vatican. Big Bill told his host, "I'll go in and have an audience with the pope and then he and I will come out on the balcony together. That should be proof that I know the pope."

Shortly Big Bill could be seen coming out on the balcony followed by a man in a tall white hat wearing a white robe. The challenger assumed he had lost his $10,000. He suddenly realized that he had never seen the pope in person and wasn't really sure that this was actually the pope. He turned to an Italian policeman in the crowd and asked, "Who is the man standing on the balcony in the tall white hat and white robe?"

"I really don't know," answered the policeman, "but the man standing next to him is Big Bill Smith from El Paso, Texas."

24 KARAT BRAGGING

While visiting an old army buddy in Kentucky, a Texan couldn't help bragging about his home state and its riches. Especially about his big ranch! "But," interrupted his buddy, thinking about Fort Knox, "we have enough gold in Kentucky to build a fence of solid gold two feet thick around your ranch!"

Not to be outdone, the Texan retorted, "Go ahead and build it. If I like it, I'll buy it!"

BUT HE DID!

There are a lot more ghost stories and folk lore tales
come out of Texas' Big Thicket than belly laughs. But
that doesn't mean the folks in that area are humorless!
One of my favorite motivational stories plays in that
area of East Texas. Perhaps the mysteries of the Big
Thicket have made its residents a little more supersti-
tious and wary of "haints" than some other folks, which
is the underlying factor of this story. This story is about
a man who worked in a sawmill, getting off work at midnight each night. Although he didn't feel real
comfortable about it, in order to save time in walking
home, he always took a shortcut through a cemetery
that was between the mill and his home.

There was a well-worn path through the graveyard,
which was some consolation. The Spanish moss-draped
oaks lent an eerie aspect to the short venture. The shad-
ows from the granite and marble angles that marked
some of the graves didn't make him very sure of himself,
even on a moonlit night.

One night, as he strode briskly through the cemetery, he didn't see the mound of dirt that marked the
freshly dug grave for tomorrow's funeral. He fell head-
long into the six-foot hole! For about fifteen minutes
there was nothing but flailing arms, as he struggled to
climb from his trap. Dirt flew as he tried to claw his way
to the surface.

He soon became exhausted and sunk to the bottom
of the open grave, bemoaning his predicament and pondering his fate. After gaining control of his senses, he

remembered that the path he took was, indeed, well traveled, which consoled him, realizing someone was sure to come along and find himself in the same state of affairs. "I will then boost them out, and they can then pull me out."

Sure enough, after about an hour he heard another person coming up the path, whistling as he walked. As he suspected, he was soon joined in the grave by a second victim of the open grave. Again there were flailing arms and legs as the second fellow attempted in vain to escape the dismal hole. The second man, soon became weary and slumped to one corner of the grave.

The first man, who had remained perfectly quiet, reached over and put his hand on the second man's arm and said, "Man, you can't jump out of here!"

But he did!

SOME BRAGGIN' HAS A PRACTICAL USE

Admittedly, Texans do have a bent toward bragging. But as some stories in this section illustrate, they are not limited to bragging about our grand and glorious state. Texans will brag about almost anything they have anything to do with, from the size of the biggest melon in last year's watermelon crop, to the number of rattles on the rattlesnake they killed last spring. Sometimes bragging is used for practical purposes, like "self-defense."

Such is the case of the story told in Rusk County about Willis Poovy's son, Lester, who was snickered about around the family's small town for being so dumb. The twenty-year-old boy's still being in the eighth grade didn't help his case. But, tired of his son's detractors, Willis spoke to the usual breakfast crowd at the East Texas Texaco and Café, whose owner proved to have a good sense of humor when he erected a sign out front which read, "EAT HERE AND GET GAS."

"I know you folks been pokin' fun at my boy, Lester, for being a mite slow, but his ma and me are mighty proud of that boy's progress. Last month he put together a jigsaw puzzle in two weeks that said on the box, "4 to 7 years"!

HE SHOULD A KNOWED BETTER!

A West Texas rancher stopping in Oklahoma on his way to a cattle sale in Kansas made the mistake of ordering a steak in one of Tulsa's better restaurants. After his meal was served he called the waiter over. "Do you mind closing the window, please."

"What is the matter," asked the waiter, "is there a breeze?"

"Yes," replied the Texan, "It's the third time my steak has blown off my plate!"

NO TIME FOR SHOWING OFF

The following story shows that there are times to brag about one's self and times to keep one's mouth shut. Some Texans haven't learned this yet!

During an uprising in West Texas, several citizens were convicted of inciting riots and were sentenced to be hanged. One was a ranch foreman, one was a doctor, and one held an engineer's degree from Texas A&M. On the day of the public hanging each man was led to the gallows where they were met by a priest.

The first man to be hanged was the ranch foreman. He was blessed by the priest and stepped on the trap door. The executioner pulled the lever releasing the trap door, but the door failed to spring open. The priest said to the crowd of on-lookers, "Surely, this is a sign from God that this man should be spared." The executioner agreed and the man was loosened from the noose and gleefully walked away.

The doctor stepped on the trap door where he, too, was blessed by the priest. The executioner threw the lever to spring the trap door, and once again the door refused to open. The priest told the crowd, "This is a sign from God that the man should be spared." The executioner was surprised, but agreed. The noose was removed, and the man quickly joined the crowd.

Then came the engineer. The noose was fitted around his neck and, after being blessed by the priest, he stepped on the trap door. Just as the executioner was about to throw the lever to spring the trap door, the engineer looked down at the door and said, "Just a minute, I think I see what the problem is!"

CAN YOU TOP THIS?

An oilman from Odessa was invited to tour an oil field in Saudi Arabia. His host gave him a grand tour of his country. One site the pair visited was one of the Mideast's major hospitals. The Texan found it quite modern. As a matter of fact, he was getting a little concerned that there was little he could brag about when

comparing Texas to his host country. The country was
so rich his usual boasting about Texas riches just didn't
seem appropriate. "Perhaps," he thought, "the hospital
will afford me a chance to expound on Texas' fine medical facilities." This, however, was not to be! Then they
came to the hospital's nursery. There he saw a sheik
standing at the glass window admiring the newborns.

Pausing to look, the Texas visitor asked the sheik,
"Which is yours?"

"The first two rows." answered the proud leader of a
large harem.

EVERYTHING IS BIG IN TEXAS

Because of the availability of prime beef, Texans
expect a steak to be plate-size. When visiting in a neigh-
boring state, a Texan ordered a steak in a restaurant
and was served a steak about the size of a pork chop.
Upon paying his check, the cashier asked him, "Sir, how
did you find your steak?" The Texan replied, "I just
moved a potato chip, and there it was!"

WHY TEXAS RICH FOLKS GET RICHER!

Before going to Europe on business, an Odessa, Texas oilman drove his Rolls Royce to a New York City bank and went in and asked for an immediate loan of $5,000. The loan officer, taken aback, requested collateral, and the Texan said, "Well then, here are the keys to my Rolls Royce." The loan officer promptly had the car driven into the bank's underground parking for safekeeping and gave the man $5,000.

Two weeks later the man walked into the bank and asked to settle up his loan and get his car back. "That will be $5,000 in principal and $15.40 in interest," the loan officer said. The Texan wrote out a check and started to walk away.

The loan officer said, "While you were gone, I found out you are a millionaire; why on earth would you need to borrow $5,000?" The Texan smiled, "Where else could I park my Rolls Royce in Manhattan for two weeks and pay only $15.40?"

TEXANS LOVE TO BRAG

A Texas millionaire was invited to Chicago by some developers, in an effort to entice the Texan to invest in a project. After showing the visitor the town, wining and dining him in the best restaurants, treating him to golf at Chicago's best country clubs, and throwing lavish parties in his honor, it was time for the Texan to return to Houston. Before he stepped on the plane to Texas, he thanked the hosts for their hospitality. "I want to repay you by inviting you to my 14-year-old son's 30,000-acre ranch in the Hill Country. He will treat you to a real Texas barbecue, and you can ride his Arabian horses to look over his 30,000 head of registered Angus cattle. We will fish for bass in the Guadalupe River and hunt white-tailed deer. He is very proud of his spread and his mother and I are proud that he earned it all himself."

The Chicago hosts thanked him for his invitation but asked, "What did such a young man do to earn his spread?" The Texan replied, "He got 3 A's and one B on his report card last semester!"

RICH BUT UNPREPARED!

Would you believe that an oilman in Midland went East to buy the Pennsylvania Railroad, but had to renege on the deal because his basement at home was 200 feet too short?

HIS CHOSEN PEOPLE

Folks who live in Texas, especially those who were born there, feel they were so placed by the hand of divine providence. The feeling, warranted or not, is best illustrated by the following story.

The pastor of a large Texas congregation was visiting another pastor in the state of New York. Upon entering his study he noticed a red telephone on his desk. When he asked his host what it was for, he was told the phone was a direct line to God. He politely asked if he might use it.

The New York pastor said, "Of course." The visitor talked on the phone nearly five minutes. After finishing, he asked his host, "How much do I owe you?" The New York pastor replied, "$17.50," which the visiting pastor freely paid.

On a subsequent visit to Texas, the New York pastor paid a visit to his Austin colleague. He was surprised that he, too, had a red phone on his desk. His inquiry as to what it was for brought the same response. "That is my direct line to God."

"May I please use it?" inquired the New York pastor. When finished with his fifteen-minute call, he asked, "And, how much do I owe you?"

The Austin pastor answered, "That will be thirty-five cents."

"I talked twice as long here for only 35¢."

"Yes, explained the Texas pastor; here, it is a local call!"

EVERYTHING DONE
BIG IN TEXAS

As non-Texans have come to expect, everything in Texas is done on a grandiose scale. One piece of Texas humor lives up to that expectation.

The story is told about an Ellis County lawsuit filed in the 1920s. The teller related how a small traveling circus was due to perform in Waxahachie for several days. As was customary, upon arrival in the small farming town, a parade was scheduled to give the locals a taste of what was in store for them. The parade included showing off the elephants who, as pachyderms were expected to do, formed a chain using their trunks to hold the tail of the elephant in front of him. The elephants were to march single file in the parade to the vacant field where the tents were to be erected. In order to do so, it was necessary for the parade to cross the M.K.T. railroad tracks en route to the circus location. The Dallas railroad telegrapher had been advised to signal the Waxahachie flagman to halt the "Katy" flyer train outside of town long enough for the circus to pass over the tracks. Unfortunately, the Waxahachie telegrapher failed to get the message.

About the time that part of the parade, which included the elephants, was crossing the tracks, the "Flyer" came through town at its scheduled high rate of speed. The locomotive hit the next to the last elephant killing the old bull instantly. The circus filed a negligence suit against the railroad, seeking damages in the amount of nearly $200,000 dollars. After both sides presented their case, the lawyer for the railroad, while admitting the error of the "Katy," argued that the settlement asked by the circus was too high! "After all, argued the attorney, the train only killed one elephant."

"This is true," said the lawyer for the small circus, "however, the Katy Flyer pulled the tails off twenty-six others!"

ETERNAL BRAGGING?

A couple in Houston who believed in predestination made a pact to try to make contact after death to verify their beliefs. One year to the day, following Charlie's tragic death in an automobile accident, the wife traveled to a mountain top in far West Texas to try to contact her departed husband.

"Charlie," said the wife, "this is Marie, can you hear me?" From the distance came the strong voice of her husband. "Marie, this is Charlie, I can hear you!" Elated at making contact with the past, Marie asked, Charlie, "Are you contented where you are?"

"Marie," the husband answered, "you can't believe how marvelous it is here. The gentle rolling hills are covered with grass that is green and lush. They are sometimes dotted with patches of flowers of every hue imaginable. The skies are always blue with a few puffy snow-white clouds that are fit for angel beds. The bodies here," Charlie continued, "are sleek and graceful. The rivers flow clear as alabaster."

"Oh, Charlie dear, I'm so glad you are happy up there in Heaven!"

"Who said anything about Heaven?" said Charlie. "I'm a bull in the Texas Hill Country!"

THE WILDCATTER

When creating prose about the Lone Star State, one cannot do so without touching on the oil industry.

Writing about Texas humor is no different. Stories about Texas oilmen could fill volumes. No character figures more prominently than the "wildcatter," the oil patch name given to speculator oil well drillers.

One story from the "patch" tells about the wildcatter who went to the dentist for his usual check-up. After a thorough examination, the dentist announced to the speculator, "I'm glad to report that I find nothing wrong with your teeth." To this, the wildcatter replied, "Drill anyway, I feel lucky today!"

INFLATED SELF-ESTEEM

St. Peter was interviewing a group of recently deceased applicants wishing to be admitted into Heaven. "And where do you come from?" Peter inquired of the first applicant. "California," replied the applicant. "Great," replied the gatekeeper, "proceed down the long marble hall, your room is number 14. But be very quiet when you pass room number 8," instructed Peter.

"And," St. Peter asked the second applicant, "where was your home?" "Michigan," was the reply. "Very well," said St. Peter, "your room is number 20 down the long hall. But be very quiet when you pass room number 8," he instructed.

The next candidate was asked the same question. "Missouri," was the reply. "Excellent," said the gatekeeper. "We have a room reserved for you, but be very quiet when you pass room number 8."

"Thanks," said the Missourian, "but, why must we all be quiet when we pass room number 8?"

"Because," answered St. Peter, "that is where we keep the Texans, and they think they are the only ones here!"

FIRST RULE OF TEXAS ETIQUETTE

A Houston man chastised his son for asking a stranger if he was from Texas. "Son," said the man, "you have just violated the first rule of Texas etiquette. You never ask a man if he's from Texas. If he is, he'll tell you. If he isn't, why embarrass him?"

ON RELIGION

One cannot travel the highways and byways of the Lone Star State and be irreverent! One does not visit the mountain peaks of far West Texas, the Hill Country awash in color at springtime, the evergreen forests of East Texas, or the coastal waters of the Gulf of Mexico and laugh in the face of an obvious and generous God! No, Texans do not laugh about religion, but they do find humor in some of the scenarios in and around their worship of a God that is omnipotent in Texas. It is these scenarios that are included in this book.

GETTING IN HOT WATER AT HOME

A quick way to get in hot water with the little woman is for her to overhear you telling a prospective bridegroom, "Son, remember, married life is like taking a hot shower! Once you get used to it, it's not so hot!"

CHRISTIANITY BY EXAMPLE

A padre accompanying a band of Spanish conquistadors helping to settle the Texas frontier converted a Comanche Indian. He took his new convert to a nearby stream where he baptized him. He told him, "From now on you will no longer be Big Bear. You will be Joseph. And," instructed the padre, "you will no longer eat meat on Friday, but only eat fish!"

Several weeks passed and the padre decided to visit his convert. He arrived at his tribe on Friday. He was disappointed to find Joseph eating a rabbit he had snared and roasted. He chided the convert, "I told you on Fridays you were to eat no meat."

The Indian said, "Padre I followed your example. I took the rabbit to the stream where I dipped him in the water and said, 'yesterday you were a rabbit, but today you are a fish.'"

THERE'S JUST SOMETHING SPECIAL ABOUT TEXAS COUNTRY CHURCHES!

Church-going folks who grow up in rural Texas will be the first to admit that there is a special ambiance in rural Texas churches unlike any other place of worship. They might not know what ambiance is, but they know exactly how it feels! Outsiders might not understand the atmosphere that exists, but it is easily recognized as "true Texan."

You might be in a Texas country church if. . .

1. The call to worship is "Ya'll come on in!"
2. You hear ranchers grumbling about Noah letting coyotes on the Ark.
3. The preacher says, "I'm going to ask Bubba to help take up the offering," and five guys stand up.
4. The restrooms are outside.
5. The opening day of deer season is recognized as an official church holiday!
6. A member requests to be buried in his four-wheel-drive truck because, "I ain't ever seen a hole it couldn't get me out of."
7. In the annual stewardship drive there is at least one pledge of two calves.
8. In its 100-year history, no pastor has ever had to buy meat or vegetables.
9. When it rains, everyone is smiling.
10. The choir is known as "The O.K. Chorale."
11. The pastor wears boots.
12. Four generations of one family sit together each Sunday.
13. Baptism is referred to as "branding."
14. You come to your car after services and find a bag of squash and okra waiting in the front seat.
15. There is a fund drive to build a new septic tank.
16. You miss worship one Sunday morning and by 2 P.M. you've had twenty calls about your health.

NOT EVERYTHING IS PERFECT

A recently deceased Texan found himself standing before St. Peter at the pearly gates. St. Peter made no motion directing him into Heaven, nor did he direct him to go below. The Texan just stood there with a puzzled look on his face.

In his mind he was pondering his past misdeeds. Unable to stand it any longer, he asked St. Peter, "What is the problem?"

St. Peter motioned him through the gates saying, "You can go on in, but I'm afraid you won't like it; it ain't like Texas!"

TELLIN' IT LIKE IT IS!

Although Texans have a reputation for stretching the truth, one story in my collection shows that some Texans can't even be paid to lie! The story is told that when a much-publicized Texas highwayman and train robber died, his brother went to a local pastor to persuade him to preach his brother's funeral.

Fearing the possible bad publicity, the preacher politely declined. The brother offered the preacher $10,000 to officiate at his brother's funeral. "Why do you offer so much money for what is normally a routine church function?" asked the pastor.

"Because you are a respected man of the cloth in West Texas and I have a special request. I want you to call my brother a saint," replied the brother. Badly in need of funds for repairs on the church where he was pastor, he reluctantly consented.

On the day of the service, the house was full of mourners. The pastor said, "We are here to pay our respects to 'Six-shooter' Henry Jones. Now we all know Henry was a thief, and a murderer, but, compared to his brother, Henry was a saint!"

WELL BROUGHT UP MOUNTAIN LION

A circuit riding preacher, while making his rounds in the sparsely settled Big Bend area of West Texas, rounded an outcropping of rock and came face to face with a fierce-looking mountain lion. Being in a box canyon with no escape route, the preacher was resolved to being a victim of the lion. He dismounted and fell to his knees in prayer.

He was shocked to see the lion fall to his knees in a prayerful stance. The preacher spoke softly to him saying, "What a Christian thing to do, to offer up a prayer for me."

"Offer a prayer for you?" said the lion. "I was brought up to say grace before each meal!"

COMMON SENSE

A story that portrays not only the wit, but the wisdom of the stereotype Texan is about a circuit riding preacher who made his way to a small West Texas community. Although usually greeted by an enthusiastic crowd, as a result of bleak, cold weather, only a handful of parishioners showed up for the Sunday morning service. Although the crowd was sparse, the well-prepared and verbose preacher spoke for nearly two hours.

At the close of the service, one honest but disgruntled rancher chided the preacher for his long-winded sermon. Noting the man's weather-beaten hands and face, the preacher made a feeble attempt at self-defense. "I see that you are a rancher," to which the man replied that he was. The preacher continued, "I know there are times when you find it necessary to feed your stock in the pasture, don't you?" Again the rancher agreed. "After you have loaded your truck with feed and arrived at the feeding place, if you a few head of cattle show up you still feed them, don't you?"

"Yes!" acknowledged the rancher, and then, in his hard-earned Texas wisdom, he added, "But I don't pump the whole load!"

POSITIVE THINKING

One of my favorite stories, which illustrates that thinking big starts very early in Texas, is about a Dallas preacher who asked a young boy, "Do you know what happens to little boys who skip church to stay home and play football?"

The small boy quickly answered, "Yes, if they do it often enough they may eventually get good enough to play for the Dallas Cowboys and make a ton of money."

OUT OF THE MOUTHS OF BABES

One South Texas community had no church house, although it did have a former minister who lived in the area. After several years without holding regular worship services, the minister convinced the men of the community that a meeting house was necessary. He said that if they would pool their resources and labor to help him build a small church, he would preach regularly for only what free will contributions were given.

The men, at the urging of their wives, worked through much of the year, when they could be spared from their crops, and built a small church. Dedication was set for a cold November day, at the first service held in the building. The preacher, as well as the community, was thrilled at the prospects of having a worship place.

A small wooden collection box was made and installed at the back of the church so that those attending could make their contributions as they entered. When the day of the first service finally came, the preacher, along with his ten-year-old son, arrived at the church early. As they entered, the preacher, wanting to set a good example for his son, reached in his pants pocket and took out a half dollar, which he dropped into the collection box.

After the service ended, the preacher, holding his son's hand, went to the back of the church. He opened the collection box and removed its contents. All that was in the box was the fifty cents he had dropped in. Obviously disappointed, he looked sadly at the boy and said, "Hard as I worked, all that I get is fifty cents!" To this

47

the boy looked sadly at his daddy and said, "Didn't you always tell me 'You only get out of life what you put into it!'"

THE LORD GIVETH, THE LORD TAKETH AWAY!

A Baptist deacon in Waco advertised a cow for sale.

"How much are you asking for your cow?" asked a prospective buyer.

"A hundred fifty dollars," said the advertiser.

"And how much milk does she give?"

"Four gallons a day," he replied.

"How do I know she will actually give that amount?" asked the purchaser.

"Oh, you can trust me," reassured the advertiser, "I'm a Baptist deacon."

"I'll take the cow," said the purchaser. "Let me take the cow home and bring the money back later. You can trust me, I'm a Presbyterian elder."

When the deacon arrived home he asked his wife, "What's a Presbyterian elder?"

"Oh," she explained, "a Presbyterian elder is the same as a Baptist deacon."

"Oh, dear," mumbled the deacon, "I have just lost my cow!"

THE DEEPER THE BETTER?

Dallas man to Austin friend…

"Do you know why Texas politicians are buried twelve feet deep instead of the usual six feet?"

"No, why?"

"Because down deep, they really are good people!"

OFF TO A BAD START

One of Fort Worth's larger churches hired a new minister who had come highly recommended as an eloquent speaker. Delivering a speech at a welcoming banquet in his honor at a local hotel, the new minister told several anecdotes which he expected to repeat at forthcoming meetings at his new church. Because he wanted the jokes to be fresh when he repeated them, he asked any reporter covering the banquet to omit the jokes from the accounts they might turn in to their newspapers. One cub reporter from the *Star Telegram*, in commenting on the new minister's speech, ended his piece with the following: "The minister told a number of stories, which cannot be published."

THE SPIRIT IS WILLING, BUT THE FLESH IS WEAK!

Texas is proud of being a part of the Southern "Bible Belt," and its abundance of religious denominations are indicative of its people's bent toward religion. Normally a person's religious beliefs are not causes for ridicule, however, the Baptists, because of their restriction of some practices, particularly their ban on consumption of alcoholic beverages, are sometimes the object of humor. Such is the case I was told about that happened in the Dallas suburb of Mesquite.

We were told that to welcome a new Methodist pastor who was moving to town, the town's close-knit ministerial alliance decided to give the new arrival a party, inviting all the town's clergy to get acquainted. Because of the season, it was decided to have a watermelon party. When the preachers all gathered at one of the minister's homes, the cooled melons were cut on the drain board in the man's kitchen. In reaching for some plates in the cabinet above, the host knocked over an open bottle of bourbon, which he kept for medicinal purposes. The liquor spilled over both cut melons.

It was too late to purchase more melons, so the host decided to serve the whiskey-tainted melons. Having a degree in psychology, he thought this an excellent way to observe how each of the clergymen reacted to the unusual melons. He watched as both the Catholic and the Lutheran pastors ate their melon as if nothing was different! The Methodist took the first bite, grimaced a bit, and continued eating, grimacing after each bite. The

Baptist pastor was really going after his and was seen putting the seeds in his coat pocket!

TEXANS TO THE CORE, DOLLAR-WISE

The minister of a little church I attended in Fort Worth was concerned about how he was going to ask the congregation for more money than they were expecting for repairs to the building. Although generous, Texans still don't cotton to fund drives. But they know how to raise money when needed.

The minister was agitated when he learned that the regular organist was sick, as he had counted on some inspirational music to stir the congregation to giving. Today, he learned there was to be a substitute organist. The minister advised the new organist to be thinking of soul-stirring music to precede his plea for additional funds.

During the services the minister paused and said, "Brothers and Sisters, we are in great difficulty! Our church repairs are going to cost twice as much as we had planned for. We need $4,000 more. Any of you who can pledge $100 or more stand up!" At that moment the substitute organist played "The Star Spangled Banner."

And that is how the substitute organist came to be our permanent organist!

"I SHOULDN'T HAVE TO TELL YOU!"

A pastor of a small South Texas town, in order to get a little added income, contracted to paint the small frame church used by the little flock he pastored. After he got nearly finished and was preparing to paint the tall steeple that topped the place of worship, he discovered he didn't order enough paint. Realizing that if he bought additional paint he would clear very little profit, and realizing that the height of the steeple made it nearly impossible for his parishioners to see, he decided to thin the remaining paint with thinner to make it go farther. Doing this, he was able to finish the job without additional cost. As he painted the steeple with the thinned-down paint, he could see that the white paint barely covered the exposed wood.

"But," he thought, "from down there the folks won't be able to see the wood showing through." Just as he finished, a huge dark cloud appeared over the church and a pouring rain came down in torrents. The pastor was dismayed to see the thin white paint running down the steeple. This was sure to expose his deceptive paint job. "What shall I do?" he cried aloud.

From the dark cloud came a booming voice, "Repaint, and thin no more!"

JUST LIKE LIVING IN TEXAS!

A hard-working Texan who had made a fortune in the lumber business was stricken with a fatal disease. When the doctor told him he had only a few weeks to live, he asked to see his pastor. Although he had much faith in God, he had always depended on his accumulated wealth to see him through a crisis. His pastor told him that he should know that he couldn't take his

wealth with him when he died. The Texan was most disappointed that, as hard as he had worked, he would be
deprived of his wealth in Heaven. He started offering up
daily prayer to God to permit him to take his wealth
with him. His fervent prayer produced positive results!

One night in his sleep, God came to him and told
him, "Because you are a self-made man and have
worked so hard for your wealth. I'll permit you to take
all you can carry in one suitcase into Heaven." The
Texan was overjoyed and as soon as he could go home
from the hospital, he had all his wealth converted into
gold bullion.

He then took his largest suitcase and packed it to the
brim with gold ingots. He now felt like he could be
happy for eternity, having his wealth around him. The
Texan, as predicted, died shortly and showed up at the
pearly gates with one suitcase. St. Peter checked his list
and was prepared to admit him. Then he told him he
could not bring in any possessions. "But," said the
Texan, "I have a special agreement with God that I
could bring in one suitcase containing my most precious
possessions." St. Peter left and was gone for a few
minutes.

Upon his return he said, "You do, indeed, have permission to bring in one suitcase containing your choice
of wealth. But, I need for you to open the suitcase so I
can see what you've brought." The Texan opened his
suitcase revealing the gold bars. The famous gatekeeper
looked at the man, quizzically.

"You brought pavement?"

GIMMIE THAT
OLD-TIME RELIGION

Formal religion, like all other things in the Republic
of Texas, included some pretty rustic settings. In the
summer months, many protestant denominations had
what was known as "protracted meetings." This was
when a preacher, known for his "saving power," was
arranged for to come to a particular congregation to
preach nightly, seven nights a week, concentrating on
converting sinners and bringing in new members.

Because of the summer heat, nearly all services were
held in the night, outside under what was called "brush
arbors." The men of the congregation cut tree limbs,
which were erected to form a support, with limbs laid
loosely on top. Scrub brush was then cut and laid on the
roof made of limbs. This gave enough ventilation for
comfort, while keeping out rain. Church pews were
arranged under the arbor and nightly preaching and
singing was conducted like a regular church. Church
members attended the brush arbor meetings in wagons
and by horse and buggy.

It is said that at such a meeting in Bell County,
attended by the Harvey family, an incident occurred
which haunted the visiting preacher for years. The
Harvey's had several boys who were known as mis-
chief-makers. As country boys, they had wildlife as pets.
On the closing night of the protracted meeting, one of
the Harvey boys asked his pa if he could take his pet
'possum with him to church. Willing to do almost anything to get the boys to church, Mr. Harvey agreed to

the request... With the understanding that the boy would maintain strict control of the animal!

Sometimes toward the end of the service the 'possum gnawed through the string that secured him to the pew that the Harvey boys occupied.

Prior to the service, the preacher had arranged to have a portion of the brush pushed back from the roof to "reveal the starry heavens, for a special big finish."

At the conclusion of the sermon, one last song was sung and the parson told the assembled worshipers, "This being our last night of a wonderful meeting, I asked a space be left open revealing the heavens in all its beauty! I would like all of you as we have our closing prayer to lift your heads and look at the Lord's starry creation." As the preacher himself lifted his head to gaze on the stars, he said, "Now lift your voices to God and say..., My God, what a rat!"

NOBODY IS PERFECT

A circuit-riding preacher in West Texas went to another minister with a problem. "I need your advice," said the preacher. "Someone stole my horse and I think it was one of my parishioners. I had the horse tied in front of my church, and Sunday afternoon when I went back to get him he was gone. I really don't know how to handle this delicate matter. What do you advise?"

The other minister listened with a sympathetic ear. "What I would do is try to appeal to the thief's con-science. Next Sunday why don't you preach on the Ten

Commandments. Really bear down on 'Thou shalt not steal'! Perhaps, if one of your members did take your horse, he'll be touched by the seriousness of his sin and bring it back."

The following week the circuit-riding preacher was seen leaving town on his horse to make his rounds. His minister friend saw him. "I see you got your horse back. Did the sermon do the trick?"

"Yes, thanks to you I'm back on my horse. I preached on the Ten Commandments, and really came down hard on 'Thou shalt not steal' When I got to 'Thou shalt not commit adultry,' I remembered where I left my horse."

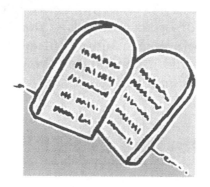

A STETSON CAN SERVE MANY PURPOSES

In a church in Lubbock an usher noticed a man wearing his big Stetson during church. He walked down and asked the man to remove his hat. "Thank goodness," said the man. "I thought that would do it. I've been visiting this church for months, and you're the first person who has spoken to me!"

IT'S RESULTS THAT COUNTS!

One Monday morning, all the weekend casualties were lined up at the pearly gates awaiting their entrance interviews. At the head of the line was a swarthy-complexioned guy in mirrored sunglasses and dressed in a brilliantly colored sport shirt and tan colored slacks. "And," asked St. Peter, "I need to know who you are so I can check my list of expected arrivals."

"My name is Hussain Mohammed, and I was a taxi driver in Houston."

"Yes," said the gatekeeper, "I see you on my list, take this golden staff and silken robe and go right in!"

The second man in line was an elderly man with white hair. "My name is William Snow and I was pastor of the St. Agatha's church for forty-two years."

"Here is your name right here," said St. Peter. "Now take this wooden staff and silken robe and enter into the joys of eternal Heaven."

"Thank you," replied the pastor, "but the guy ahead of me was a taxi driver and he got a gold staff. Why do I get only a wooden one?"

"Pastor, the fact is, all those years you preached, people slept, but the taxi driver, with Houston's traffic conditions scared the hell outta more people daily than you did in 42 years of preaching!"

ON POLITICS

Politics and politicians are very much a serious part of our democratic way of life. Yet, like religion, while serious, it can, on occasion, be as funny as a circus clown in full greasepaint. One can turn to the editorial page of most major newspapers and find an editorial cartoon lampooning the political exploits of the times. Politicians have, by their conduct, presented themselves as the butt of innumerable jokes! Much to the delight of the cartoonists who make their living caricaturing these public servants and their exploits. Texas politics and politicians provide an especially fertile field for collecting humor, as they, like many things done in Texas, are magnified out of proportion!

TEXAS POLITICIANS, LIKE ATTORNEYS, ENJOY A PARTICULAR IRREVERENCE

Three men traveling through Texas by car sought a place to spend the night. One man was a rabbi, one was from India, and the driver was a Texas politician. The visiting rabbi suggested to their host, the driver, that, because of their reputation for friendliness, perhaps a local farmer would give them a room in their home? The Texan stopped the car and approached the door of a nearby farm in Central Texas.

After they explained their difficulty in finding a place to stay, the farmer indicated that the three men would be welcome to stay at his home, but his extra room had only two beds. He told them that one man could sleep in his nearby barn, which he assured them was warm and comfortable. The rabbi said that he would be glad to sleep in the barn, where there was sure to be hay.

A short time after he had left the other two men, they heard a knock at the door. Opening the door they saw the rabbi had returned. He said he was sorry but he could not sleep in the barn as there was a pig in the barn, which was unclean to a Jew. With this, the man from India said he would be glad to sleep in the barn.

But, as was the case with the rabbi, he returned shortly and announced that he could not sleep in the barn, as there was a cow in the barn, and in his country cows were sacred, "and I am not worthy to sleep in the same room with a cow."

The Texas politician told both men that he had no religious leanings at all and would be glad to sleep in the barn with the cow and pig. The two had barely gotten in bed when they heard a knock at the door. Upon opening the door, they saw the cow and pig standing in the hall.

AT LEAST HE DID HIS JOB

Not all Texas politicians are steeped in scandal and abuse of power. At least one office-holder in South Texas can brag about his tenure in office. "I was," he bragged to a friend, "elected dog catcher in my town for two years, but I lost my job."

"Change of mayors?" asked his listener.

"No," answered the politician, "I finally caught the dog."

HOOF IN MOUTH DISEASE

To prove the point that Texas humor spared no victims, one need only to recall to memory what may have been the most humorous faux pas in Texas politics. This political error was made by former governor Jim Ferguson, after being embroiled in a scandal that resulted in his impeachment, coupled with resignation from office, on the heels of a grand jury indictment listing seven counts of misapplication of public funds, one count of embezzlement, and one count of diversion of public funds.

In a subsequent bid for reelection to public office, "Farmer Jim," as he was known, included the following statement in a campaign speech, "Two years ago, you elected the best governor money could buy."

A critic of "Farmer Jim" might have termed this as the politician's most truthful speech!

TEXAS, A TWO-PARTY STATE

The difficult transition of Texas into a two-party state is illustrated by this story. A man jogged each weekend in his neighborhood. One Saturday morning he jogged by a small boy sitting on a corner with a cardboard box and a hand-lettered sign that read "Puppies for sale." The man looked in the box and saw a litter of newborn puppies. The man asked the boy, "What kind of puppies are they?"

"These are Democrat puppies," answered the boy.

"Well," said the man, "my wife is the dog lover in the family; if you are going to be here next Saturday, I'll bring her with me to have a look." Assured that he would be there, the man jogged away.

The following Saturday the man returned with his wife. "And," asked the lady, "What kind of dogs are they?"

"They are Republican dogs," replied the small boy.

"Wait a minute," said the man, "last week you told me the dogs were Democrat dogs."

"Yes," answered the boy, "but in the meantime they got their eyes open!"

BEING A TEXAS POLITICIAN CAN BE A BREEZE

A Houstonian passed away and found himself standing at the pearly gates, in the presence of St. Peter. The gatekeeper spoke first. "It's a very slow day in Heaven, would you like to take a tour of our kingdom?"

"Of course," replied the Texan.

St. Peter took the new arrival to a large room that was filled with snow-white wings. "This," he explained, "is where we issue the angels their wings."

Next, the pair visited a very long golden hall, which had harps hanging on the walls. "This hall is where the angels are issued their harps."

The following room visited by the Saint and the new arrival was a most unusual room. The four walls were covered with clocks. There were hundreds of millions of them, noted the Houstonian.

"Why so many clocks," asked the Texan.

"This," said the gatekeeper, "is where we keep up with all the lies told on earth. Everyone on earth has a clock, and every time they tell a lie the minute hand turns back one minute."

"But," inquired the Texan, looking up, "why do you have that giant clock on the ceiling?"

"That," answered the Saint, "is the clock for your Texas governor. We sometimes use it as a ceiling fan!"

THE MIRACLE OF POLITICS

A preacher holding a revival in a West Texas town was debating an oilman who doubted the miracle of divine chastisement. "Let me tell you of a remarkable occurrence," the preacher said. "In this morning's paper there is an article about a Texas politician who was struck by lightning while he was lying. Miraculous incident don't you think?"

"I don't know," said the oilman, "be more of a miracle if lightning struck a Texas politician when he wasn't lying!"

POLITICIANS ARE ALWAYS FAIR GAME

When Lyndon B. Johnson worked his way from the Texas Hill Country to the White House, many Texans, even his supporters, felt that he had been pushed into the highest office by his wife, "Lady Bird." As a result, some of the good ol' boys felt little compassion for the "pushy" role "Bird" had taken in the Texan's life.

An example of this is a joke that was going around while Lyndon was in office. It was said that a Texas preacher preached a sermon on "Love." He said we are supposed to love everybody. One member of the church spoke up and asked, "What if you don't like someone?"

"Who is it you don't love?" asked the preacher.

"Well, I don't love the president," answered the member.

The preacher said, "Don't you realize that the president is only in office because of a higher power?"

"Yeah, I know," said the member, "and I don't care much for her, neither!"

YOU CAN'T FOOL ALL THE PEOPLE ALL THE TIME

During one presidential election year when Lyndon Johnson was a candidate for the presidency, it was arranged for him to speak to a tribe of Native Americans on their Texas reservation. His entourage was pleasantly surprised that the tribe's preparation had included their erecting a large platform in a field where they pastured their herd of cattle. This would enable Mr. Johnson to speak to the entire tribe after meeting with their chief and council of elders. The candidate mounted the platform and made a rousing speech.

"If I am elected," he said, "I will establish a totally new Indian agency dedicated to the welfare of the modern Native American!" His opening remarks were greeted with an obviously well orchestrated cheer, "kasaba, kasaba!"

He continued, "I shall see that every Native American has his own home in which he can raise his family." Once again a mighty shout went up from the tribe massed before him, "kasaba, kasaba!"

Continuing, Mr. Johnson promised, "If elected I will see that every Indian boy and girl has free schooling." "Kasaba, kasaba!" shouted the throng of Indians.

As the candidate was escorted across the pasture to his waiting limousine, one of the tribe's braves, assigned to escort him, turned to him and said, "Watch out, Mr. Johnson, don't step in the kasaba!"

HE'S ONLY HUMAN!

One year, for his birthday, the then president Lyndon Johnson invited several members of the Republican Congress to his Johnson City ranch on the Pedernales River for a Texas-style barbecue. On the day of the party, two of the opposition's senators arrived just in time to see President Johnson come out on the huge porch. They stopped their car short of crossing the river.

Upon seeing the arriving guests, Johnson started walking down the vast yard toward the river. The two guests watched as, upon reaching the banks of the Pedernales, Johnson continued to walk across the water. When he was about halfway across, one senator said to his colleague in Congress, "See, he can walk on water!"

"Yes," said the other Republican, "but I was here last year, and he knows where the stumps are!"

TEXAS POLITICIAN'S PHILOSOPHY ON FENCE STRADDLING

The only things in the middle of the road are yellow stripes and dead armadillos.

ON TEXAS PRIDE

Just as Texas cattle can be identified by the brand that is indelibly etched into their hides, the state's residents, particularly its native sons, are easily identified by their outspoken pride, not only in their state, but in themselves!

We are proud of our diverse cultures, our hard won independence, and our heritage. This pride is sometimes translated into a distinct personal independence!

This personal independence is as vital to the individual as independence from foreign rule was to its early Anglo settlers. This bent for independence and pride sometimes shines through in a way that is very humorous. These few stories are excellent examples of Texas pride.

BOOM AND BUST IN TEXAS

Pride in Texas is not darkened one whit by bad times. Everything in Texas is bigger. And so it is with booms and busts. Good times in Texas can be very good, and the hard times can be terrible. But even during the hard times, Texans show their optimism.

A Texas politician was once asked by a reporter about an economic recession. To the asking reporter the politically savvy politician replied, "We don't have recessions in Texas. But I must admit, this is the worst boom we've had in years."

EVERY CLOUD HAS A SILVER LINING

Two men who had been neighbors in Austin met at a convention in Dallas. "Haven't seen you since our golf game last year. How have things gone with you this past year?"

"Catastrophic!" replied the former neighbor.

"What happened?" asked his friend.

"My twenty-five-year-old daughter, Sally, married a Yankee," explained the Austinite. "My wife must have turned over in her grave! But," he continued, "that's only the beginning."

"What else made things so terrible?" inquired his friend.

"The guy has a brother who is as good looking as any movie star, and my younger daughter is engaged to him."

"Good!" replied his friend.

"What do you mean, good?" asked the neighbor.

"Well," replied his friend, "at least your wife will be right-side up in her grave again!"

PROPHECY COMES TRUE

A Texan dies and goes to hell. While down there, the devil notices that he is not suffering like the rest. He checks the gages and sees that it's 90 degrees and about 80 percent humidity. He asks the Texan why he's so happy.

The Texan says, "I like it here; it's just like Texas in June." The devil goes over and turns up the temperature to 100 degrees and the humidity to 90 percent.

After turning everything up he goes looking for the Texan. He finds him standing around unbuttoning his shirt, just as happy as he can be. The devil quizzes the Texan again as to why he's so happy. The Texan says, "This is even better, it's like Texas in July, my favorite month." The devil, now upset, decides to really make the Texan suffer. He goes over and turns the heat up to 120 degrees and the humidity to 100 percent.

"Now, let's see what the Texan is up to," he says. So he goes looking for the Texan. He finds him taking his shirt off, even happier than before. Unable to figure it out, the devil once again asks why he's so happy.

"This is fine, it's just like Texas in August."

"That's it, I'll get this guy." He goes over and turns the temperature down to a freezing 25 degrees. "Let's see what the Texan says about this." The devil looks around and finds the Texan jumping for joy and yelling.

"The Rangers finally won the World Series," said the Texan.

"And," asked the devil, "how would you know, being down here?"

"My friends always said the Rangers would win the World Series when hell freezes over," replied the jubilant Texan.

PRIDE STARTS YOUNG IN TEXAS

During one Texas boy's first year in school, the teacher asked if he knew where babies come from. "Sure," answered Billy, without hesitation. "Babies come from Sears and Roebuck!" The boy's teacher called the boy's mother and told her what little Billy had said.

When Billy got home from school that day his mother asked him, "Why did you tell the teacher that babies come from Sears and Roebuck?"

"Mother, I didn't want the other kids to know that we were so poor we had to make our own babies!"

TEXAS FARMERS HAVE A HARD ROW TO HOE!

A Texas farmer included in his will that he wanted six of his creditors for pallbearers when he died. He explained, "They have been carrying me most of my life; they may as well finish the job."

PRIDE CAN BE A DANGEROUS THING

Nearly every home in Texas (perhaps a carryover from frontier days) has a gun of some description. And boys learn to safely use them at an early age. They develop an eagerness to show off their prowess with a gun, as is understandable.

They take great pride in demonstrating this innate skill with a gun. But, a little pride can be a dangerous thing. Perhaps this is why pride is listed among the deadly sins in the Bible! One Mills County lad learned this at an early age. He borrowed his father's shotgun one Saturday afternoon and returned that same evening. He was beaming with pride when he announced to his father that he had killed two big fat ducks.

"Were they wild?" asked his daddy.

"No," said the boy, "but the farmer they belonged to was really wild!"

TEXAS INDEPENDENCE

Although well known for their friendliness, Texans covet their independence both collectively and individually. This is clearly illustrated by this story.

A young boy was sitting on a curb in a small Texas town eating chocolate bars. He was observed stuffing bars into his mouth as fast as he could unwrap the candy.

A man approached the chocolate-smeared boy and said, "Young man, I've been watching you stuff your face full of chocolate as fast as you could unwrap the bars. Don't you know you are shortening your life by eating so much chocolate? Every bite of chocolate you eat makes your life a little shorter!"

The boy looked the man squarely in the eyes and said, "My grandfather lived to be a hundred and eight."

"By eating chocolate?" inquired the man.

"No," answered the boy. "By minding his own business!" The well-intentioned man turned and walked away.

PATRIOT TO THE END

On an airplane trip to Europe, the passengers included a Texan, a Mexican, a Frenchman, and an Englishman. The aircraft had barely gotten over the Atlantic when the pilot frantically dashed into the passenger compartment and announced that the plane had lost one engine. He instructed the passengers to throw out all unnecessary baggage to lighten the load so that the plane could avoid a crash landing. After this was done, the craft leveled out for a while but was obviously not flying at full altitude.

Another visit by the captain caused a stir when he announced that the plane was still too heavy. "One of you, I'm afraid, must sacrifice your life by jumping, or we will lose all passengers." The proud Englishman was the first to volunteer. The emergency door was opened and the Englishman shouted, "God save the king!" and leapt from the plane.

Hardly had the remaining passengers recovered from this brave act, until the captain reappeared and announced the loss of a second engine. "Again, someone will have to leave the plane to assure the saving of the rest." The Frenchman stepped to the emergency door and, with a shout of "Vive la France!" leapt into the Atlantic.

But, the appearance of the captain once again brought more bad news. The loss of a third engine necessitated the need for the loss of more weight. With this, the Texan opened the emergency door, and loudly shouting, "Remember the Alamo!" threw out the Mexican.

THERE ARE NO SACRED COWS IN TEXAS HUMOR

One thing is certain about Texas humor, when it comes to getting a laugh there are no sacred cows! Even the heroes of Texas history, who are considered icons, may at times be sacrificed on the alter of Texas humor.

Such is the case in the story of "Old Sam," The setting for this story is on South Main Street, near Hermann Park, in Houston, Texas. On a small island of grass at that location stands a magnificent bronze equestrian statue of General Sam Houston, who gave Texas its independence from Mexico by defeating General Santa Anna at nearby San Jacinto Battleground.

Houston sits astride his favorite mount and his arm, it is said, points in the general direction of the battlefield. Locals tell of a young couple who were transferred to Houston from the East Coast by the husband's company. The couple adjusted well to the move. Their six-year-old son, however, fretted because he had to move away from his friends. In an effort to help make up for the loss and help him make new friends, the couple decided to bring him to Hermann Park, which his father, a Houstonian by birth, knew about.

While at the park, the boy noticed the statue. He asked his father to take him for a closer look. The Texan father did so with great pride.

The boy asked, "Whose statue is that, Dad?"

"Son," answered the father, "that's Old Sam." The small boy became enamored of the statue, to the point that each weekend he forgot about the swings and other playthings at the park and begged, instead, to be taken directly to see "Old Sam." This scenario continued week after week, much to the satisfaction of his Texas-born father.

Then came the day dreaded by the couple. The parents had to tell their son that they were being transferred back to the East Coast. The little boy's first reaction was, "Will you take me back, one last time, to see Old Sam?" The small boy stood solemnly in front of the tribute to the great Texan. "Bye, Old Sam, bye, Old Sam," said the boy in a quivering voice. Then he turned to his proud father and asked, "Dad, who is that riding Old Sam?"

ON FOOTBALL
LOYALTY IN TEXAS

Dwight Eisenhower, born in Denison, Texas, is quoted as saying, "An atheist is a guy who watches the Notre Dame-SMU game and doesn't care who wins."

TEXANS WILL BE TEXANS

A truck driver, who lived north of Denison near the Oklahoma border, had a habit of hitting "Okies" who crossed the border into Texas. He would watch them walk along the highway a piece and then swerve his truck and hit them. He would get great joy from the dull THUD sound it made as he hit the unsuspecting Okies.

One day while driving he saw a priest walking along the highway. He stopped and asked the priest where he was going. The priest said he was going to the little church about five miles down the highway. "Hop in," said the truck driver, "I'll take you to the church." The priest climbed in and sat in the passenger seat of the truck.

A few minutes later the truck driver saw an Okie walking down the side of the highway. He headed directly for him. Just then he remembered he had a priest in the truck and swerved his truck just in time to miss the Okie. Although he was certain he had missed the man, he heard the telltale THUD! Looking in his rear view mirror he saw nothing.

He turned to the priest and said, "Father, did you see that?, I almost hit that Okie."

"Yes," said the priest, "but I got him with my door!"

ON "OUTSIDERS"

Many non-Texans, many of which we call "Yankees," find much to laugh about when they are exposed for any length of time to Texans and our way of life, our "twangy" talk, our expressions, and our dress. Watching outsiders as they try to adjust to being in Texas and with Texans affords us as many laughs as we afford them! The relationship of "outsiders" with Texans has always spawned some humorous moments. These stories are just a few samples of how these two cultures viewed one another.

AS SEEN THROUGH OTHERS' EYES

Some of our best Texans are transplants. Such is the case of my good friend Bob Neff, who comes to Texas courtesy the U.S. Air Force. This former, and he proudly emphasizes "former," New Yorker is probably more sold on Texas than many natives. Of course anyone who grew up in Buffalo, N.Y. would be! Bob fairly oozes with admiration for his friends in San Angelo and this part of the state where he was stationed. It is he who reminded us how Texans have learned to laugh at themselves. "For instance," he said, "that part of Texas is so flat they have to put up signs so the rivers will know which way to run!"

He also noted that a little further west, when the folks say they got a four-inch rain, they mean the drops were four inches apart. Bob said he couldn't believe it when, during a terrible dust storm, one farmer, who was accustomed to the undesirable condition, only remarked, "There goes one farm changing places with its neighbor."

Realizing that some Texans can be obnoxious, Bob said that when God made Texas, it was so beautiful and desirable compared to the other states, he was a little embarrassed, so he made Texans to make up for it!

Bob was not the first to note that the reason Amarillo was so cold in the wintertime was that the only thing between the Panhandle city and the North Pole was a barbed wire fence.

But, friend or not, Bob went too far when he said that the smallest thing in the world was a Texan with the bragging kicked out of him!

WHO SAID TEXANS TALK FUNNY?

A New Yorker, recently transferred to Texas by his company, was frequently heard belittling his new neighbors for their funny speech patterns.

When asked by a Texas colleague for an example of what he called "funny," he told of a recent visit to a small town's courthouse square. It was December and Christmas was nearing. The town had just erected a nativity scene. As the New Yorker walked around the manger and the familiar figures surrounding it, he noticed that the cut out figures of the three wise men all had fire hoses draped over their shoulders. He asked one of the town's officials in the courthouse, "Why do the three wise men have fire hoses draped over their shoulders?"

The official told the visitor that "the scriptures plainly say that the wise men were coming from afar!" The New Yorker made his point!

YANKEES AND THE TEXAS WAY OF LIFE

Driving through Texas a New Yorker collided with a truck pulling a horse trailer. A few months later, the New Yorker was in court trying to collect damages for injuries. "How can you claim damages for injuries," asked the lawyer for the insurance company, "when at the time of the accident, you told the police you were fine?"

The New Yorker replied, "Well, you see, I was lying in the highway in lots of pain when I heard someone say that the horse had a broken leg. The next thing I knew, the Texas Ranger who was investigating, took out his pistol and shot the horse. He then turned to me and asked me, 'How are you?' I replied, 'I'm just fine, thanks!'"

LOYALTY IS A STATE OF MIND IN TEXAS

A young man from San Antonio, who enlisted in the army, wrote home to his mother, "We have fifteen men in a room here. In my room there are ten Texans and five Yankees."

"Good," wrote back his mother, "it makes me very proud of you that you have already taken five prisoners!"

MISSING THE POINT!

A Texan, while visiting the British Isles, engaged a Brit in conversation about his country. "In Texas," bragged the Texan, "I can board a train in the morning and twenty-four hours later I will still be in Texas."

"I know what you mean, old chap," said the Londoner, "we have slow trains in England, too!"

LEARNING TEXAS FROM THE GROUND UP!

Two young New Yorkers, having heard about Texas all their lives, wanted to see the state for themselves. Having little money, they started hitchhiking across country. One ride landed them on the highway just outside of Amarillo.

Lucky for them, they were just a few feet from the fence of one of Texas' true working ranches. After looking across the huge pasture at the typical Texas scene, including a farmhouse and spinning windmill, they noticed an elderly man in work clothes bending over a cow that lay on its side near the fence.

Being curious and eager to observe Texas, they ambled along the fence until they reached the man and his cow. "Having trouble?" asked the Yankee travelers.

"A little," replied the sweating rancher.

"Can we be of help?" said the eager viewers.

"You can climb over here and help me pull this calf, if you really want to help," said the grateful rancher.

The two young New Yorkers, feeling excited to really be on a Texas ranch, climbed over the fence and helped the rancher birth the calf. When the event was finally over, the rancher said, "I thank you for your help. Now if you come to my house, we will wash up and I'll have my wife fix you some vittles." Being hungry from their travels and the unexpected work, the visitors readily accepted the rancher's hospitality. After eating, the rancher said, "Now, boys, I want to give you ten dollars for your help."

"Fine," said one of the New Yorkers, "but you can keep your money if you will only tell us one thing. How fast was that calf going when it hit that cow in the rump?"

TAKES ONE TO KNOW ONE!

A Texan, though limited in talent, had a burning desire to be in show business. Not being able to sing or dance, but being a reasonably good joke teller, the man decided to learn to be a ventriloquist. He made himself a lifelike dummy and dressed him in Western attire. Realizing he couldn't expect to start with bookings in the big theaters, he decided to try out his act in small towns. Having friends in Enid, Oklahoma, he was able to secure an engagement in a comedy club in that tiny town.

His first night was going well, as he had a good supply of funny but obviously uncomplimentary jokes about Okies. In the back a rather tall, well-built man stood and shouted, "O.K. fellow, one more joke about Oklahoma and I'm gonna cram that cowboy hat down your throat!"

The Texan smiled and said, "I'm sorry, I didn't mean to offend you."

The Okie said, "I wasn't talking to you, buddy, I was talking to the little guy on your knee."

WHO SAID THE WAR WAS OVER?

What do you call 500 Yankees at the bottom of the ocean?

Answer: A darn good start!

REMEMBER OUR STATE MOTTO "FRIENDSHIP"

Sometimes Texas humor goes out of its way to perpetuate the imagery of the roughness and the toughness of its land and citizens—at least as perceived in the minds of non-Texans. An example is the story of a West Texan who owns a small spread near El Paso.

He received a letter from an old army buddy who lived in New York. His pal was coming through Texas on a business trip and wanted to stop off and see a real ranch. The Texan, as can be expected, extended an invitation. After the "tenderfoot" arrived, the rancher offered to show him the ranch by horseback. They had only ridden a few hundred yards when the New Yorker saw his first rattlesnake.

Only minutes later the second rattler appeared. Shortly the third ominous-looking rattlesnake appeared. The New Yorker commented on the proliferation of the venomous reptiles. The Texan agreed that these dangers had to be overcome on a daily basis.

"If you should be bitten on the arm or hand," asked the visitor, "what would you do?" The rancher explained how one must take a knife, cut across the fang wounds, suck the poison out, and spit it on the ground! "And," inquired the New Yorker, "what if you were bitten on the leg?" The rancher repeated the procedure for the visitor. "Supposed you are bitten on your rear end?" asked his guest.

"Then," said the Texan, "that's when you find out who your friends are!"

BUT YOU DON'T HAVE TO SHOVEL THE HEAT!

As a native Texan, I am constantly amazed at newly arrived Yankees (folks from north of the Red River, except "Okies") who make jokes about our heat in the

summer. Surely, if their companies had transferred them to the Sahara Desert, instead, wouldn't they expect to find sand in their shoes periodically, or smell camel's breath now and then? Or even find a sheik living on their block?

The following are a few snide remarks intercepted from censored mail back home to friends in Chicago: "You know you are in Texas when..."

- You discover that in July it takes only two fingers to drive your car.
- You no longer associate bridges with water or rivers.
- You can say 110 degrees without fainting.
- You eat hot chili to cool your mouth off.
- You can make sun tea instantly!
- You learn that seat belts make pretty good branding irons.
- The best parking spaces are determined by shade, not distance.
- Hotter water comes from the cold water tap than the hot one.
- In July, kids are on summer vacation and not one person is on the street.
- You get second degree burns opening the car door.
- Sunscreen is sold year round.
- No one would dream of putting vinyl upholstery in a car.
- Your biggest fear when riding a bicycle is that you have a wreck and get knocked unconscious and lay on the street and get cooked to death.

Remember one thing, you tenderfoots, *You don't have to shovel heat!!!*

TEXAS' UNKINDEST INSULT

What most Texans would consider "fightin' words" is attributed to Gen. Philip H. Sheridan. In 1867, following the Civil War, the general was made Military Governor of the Fifth Military District consisting of Louisiana and Texas. On July 30, 1867, after removing several Texas officials from office, "because they were detriments to Reconstruction," Sheridan's harsh policies of Reconstruction met with the disapproval of President Andrew Johnson, who removed Sheridan from office as a tyrant.

Perhaps influenced by his being stationed in Texas, Sheridan is attributed with making the statement, "If I owned hell and Texas, I'd live in hell and rent Texas out"!

HOW TO SHUT UP A TEXAN

An Australian rancher was visiting a Texas ranch to try to get some ideas about managing his ranch back home. Every time he tried to extol the virtues of his Australian ranch, the Texan always interrupted by bragging that everything in Texas was "twice as big." When the visit was complete, the Australian insisted that his Texas host make a trip to Australia to see the country for himself, especially his ranch in the outback.

The Texan agreed and a date was set. Upon his arrival, the Aussie and the Texan mounted up to tour the ranch. Not long after they started, they encountered the first kangaroo the Texan had ever seen. It jumped along the fence row at sixty miles an hour, leaping the length of the distance between two fence posts at a time.

The action continued for about a mile and the Texan could stand it no more. "What," he asked, "is that?"

"That, my friend, is a grasshopper. I guess you've got them twice that big in Texas?"

JEALOUSY PERSONIFIED

One Eastern newspaperman who came through Texas for the first time later reported that "A tornado swept through one Texas town doing one million dollars worth of improvements!"

TEXAS, LAND OF PLENTY

My German friend, Karl Kuby of Dallas, knows what he is talking about when he tells the story about two Europeans who, upon hearing about the opportunities in the Lone Star State, decide to immigrate to Texas. Getting off the airplane at the Dallas-Fort Worth International Airport, they take a taxi to the heart of Dallas, where they begin to walk the busy streets to just look at its wonders.

"Just look at those magnificent tall buildings," said one of the Europeans as they walked down Elm Street admiring the sights and sounds of the city. One looked down and saw a $20 bill lying on the sidewalk. "You see," he remarked to his friend, "just as we were told, the streets *are* paved with gold in Texas." Just as he was bending over to pick up the money, his friend said, forcefully, "Don't pick it up!"

"And why not?" inquired the newly arrived immigrant.

"Let's not work on our first day here!" said his friend confidently.

MODERNIZING THE OLD WEST

Being an outsider is not limited to those from areas outside Texas! We who were born and raised in the larger cities of Texas are generally as separated from the lifestyles of farmers and ranchers as those whom we call "back-Easterners." This chasm was vividly pointed out to me recently at the National Cowboy Symposium in Lubbock when a working cowboy from a nearby ranch told how he was asked to speak to a class of elementary school children in one of West Texas' larger cities. He decided to take some of a cowboy's working gear to show to the young people. He settled on a pair of his prized silver spurs. Holding up the spurs, he asked if anyone knew what they were. In unison the class all answered, "spurs."

"And," he asked, "who knows what spurs are used for?" One bright-looking boy about twelve years old held up his hand.

The cowboy asked the boy what the spurs were used for. The boy, without a second thought, answered, "To jump-start your horse with!"

ON MARRIAGE

Humor, by its very definition, should not be dangerous. As is the case in this book, even in the midst of a
Texas summer, one is skating on thin ice when passing
on jokes about the sanctity of marriage. The risk is the
nearness of the antagonist. The same holds true of
mother-in-law jokes. In Texas the risks are no less, but
Texans, toughened up by the environment, seem to
weather the storm better! It is comforting to know that
marriage was fair game for humorists in early Texas.
Please accept these stories in the light-hearted spirit in
which they are offered.

Just be careful repeating them!

MARRIAGE GETS
ANOTHER BUM RAP

A West Texas rancher's mule kicked his wife in the head, killing her instantly. On the day of her funeral, about 300 people showed up. A neighbor remarked, "I didn't know your wife had so many friends."

The widower answered, "They ain't all her friends. Most of them are here to see about buying my mule!"

GOOD THING THE WIFE
WASN'T A LIP READER

An elderly couple was driving through Oklahoma with the wife at the wheel. They were pulled over by a highway patrolman. The trooper walked to the driver's side and asked the woman, "Do you know you were speeding?"

The woman turned to her husband and in a loud voice asked, "WHAT DID HE SAY?"

The man answered, also in a loud voice, "HE SAID YOU WERE SPEEDING."

The patrolman asked the woman for her drivers license. "WHAT DID HE SAY?" asked the woman, again in a loud voice.

The husband replied, "HE SAID HE WANTS YOUR LICENSE!" It was obvious the woman was hard of hearing.

The trooper looked at the license and said, "I see you're from Texas. I dated a woman from Texas once but gave her up, as she was the worst kisser I ever met."

The wife turned to her husband and said, "WHAT DID HE SAY?"

The husband in a loud voice replied, "HE THINKS HE KNEW YOU ONCE!"

SARCASM ALLOWED

Sometimes Texas humor takes on a biting quality; however, the humor always shows through any sarcasm exhibited. Such is the case in the story of a Texas father who was accompanying his recently engaged daughter, who was traveling by stage to her wedding in San Antonio. About halfway to her destination the stage was stopped by a robber. The highwayman demanded all the money and valuables of the stage's passengers, in addition to the strong box on the stage.

After the robbery, the father noticed that his daughter still wore her large diamond engagement ring. He asked her how she kept the robber from noticing the ring. "When I saw the robber stopping the stage, I slipped off the ring and put it in my mouth."

To this, the father replied, "Golly, if your maw had been here, I could have saved my wallet and watch!"

TWO DISTINCT POINTS OF VIEW

A man in Abilene goes into a wine shop and asks the clerk, "Have you an appropriate wine for a silver wedding anniversary?"

"That depends," replied the clerk, do you want to celebrate it or forget it?"

IF FATE HANDS YOU A LEMON, MAKE LEMONADE

Down in Navarro County, just south of Dallas, lived an old spinster by the name of Fern Moss. Miss Moss wasn't bashful about letting you know how desperate she was to find a husband. She said once while coming home from shopping in Dallas, she was stopped and robbed by a gunman. "But," she told him, "I have no money."

With that, the gunman started to frisk Fern, patting her down from head-to-toe. When finished, the gunman asked her, "You really don't have any money, do you?"

"No," said Fern, "but if you'll do that again, I'll write you a check!"

NOT ALL TEXANS ARE FEARLESS

A Texas rodeo performer was attempting to improve his skills. He decided to add steer wrestling to the events he could enter. He enlisted a good steer-wrestler to teach him the event. "First, said the teacher, you ride as fast as you can to catch up with the running steer. And then you carefully slide off your horse and take hold of the steer's horns."

Upon hearing these instructions, the student recoiled and started to shudder! "I have a terrible fear of horns," said the student.

"Don't worry," said the teacher, sympathetically. "After a few times you'll get over your fear."

"You don't understand," replied the cowboy, "I can't even stand to hear a horn!"

"What gave you such a fear of horns," asked the teacher.

"Well, you see," replied the cowboy, "A few years ago my ex-wife ran away with a truck driver. And every time I hear a horn, I'm afraid he's bringing her back!"

YOU CAN'T EXPECT CHANGE OVERNIGHT!

A Scotsman immigrated to the new frontier of Texas in the middle 1800s. Soon, he too, found himself wearing a six-gun on his hip. One evening he came home early and found his wife with another man. After ordering the two outside, the frugal Scotsman instructed them, "Now stand one behind the other, then I can kill you both with one bullet!"

THE ROLE MODEL

A mother was trying to get through her housework, but her six-year-old son Billy kept running through the house whooping like a Comanche Indian and being mischievous in general.

After the tenth time the mother said, "Billy, why can't you just be good for a while?"

To this Billy replied, "Mother, I'll be good for a dollar."

"But," said Billy's mother, "why can't you be like your father and be good for nothing?"

GETTING OFF TO A RIGHT START

Following a big South Texas wedding, the groom hitched his fine horse to the couple's buckboard to get started on their honeymoon. The horse, a bit skittish from all the wedding trappings added to the buckboard, kicked backward striking the front of the buckboard. "THAT'S ONCE!" shouted the groom as he strapped the horse a stinging blow with the reins. The horse calmed a bit and proceeded forward.

He stopped again and once again kicked with a mighty force that rocked the couple's buckboard. "THAT'S TWICE!" shouted the furious husband, as he dealt the animal another blow with the reins. This gave the horse reason to pull forward. But the progress was short-lived.

Once again, the animal balked and delivered a smashing kick backward into the buckboard. With this, the groom said, "THAT'S THREE TIMES!" and to the surprise of his bride, took his pistol from its holster and sent a bullet crashing into the horse's head.

"Why did you do that?" inquired the nervous bride.

"This," said the groom, "is a rather new horse and he has to learn who's boss!"

"But, darling, don't you think you were a little extreme?"

The groom looked his new wife straight in the eyes and said, "THAT'S ONCE!"

LIVING A DOG'S LIFE!

A young married Texan, wanting to impress his new bride, went to an architect. "My folks gave me a thousand dollars for my wedding. I want to build a new house. What kind of a house can I build for a thousand dollars?"

"Just how big is your dog?" asked the architect.

SOUR GRAPES!

When the circuit-riding preacher came through Fort Davis, one of the parishioners asked him following the sermon, "Preacher, do you think its wrong for one man to profit from another man's mistake?"

"I most certainly do," said the minister.

"Then, said the man, would you please return the five dollars I gave you for marrying me last year?"

THERE'S NO PLACE LIKE HOME!

A Uvalde rancher came to the Fort Worth stock show to buy cattle for his ranch. He stayed a week in one of the city's largest hotels. One morning he made his way to the hotel coffee shop for breakfast. The coffee the waitress brought was cold. The toast was burnt. His egg was cooked stone hard! With a smile on his face, he asked the waitress, "Would you please pull your hair down in your face and sit by me and start nagging? I've been here six days and I'm really homesick for my wife!"

BEAUTY IS IN THE EYE
OF THE BEHOLDER!

Preacher: "Does anyone know anybody who is perfect?"

A little man in the back raised his hand.

"Who," asked the preacher, "do you know that's perfect?"

Parishioner: "My wife's first husband who came from Texas!"

LAST OF THE BIG SPENDERS

OR
YOU GET WHAT YOU PAY FOR

While Texans have the reputation for flaunting their wealth, this has not always been the case.

God said he was going to give Adam a companion and it would be a woman. He said this person will wash your clothes and cook for you. She will always agree with all the decisions you make. She will bear your children and never ask you to get up in the middle of the night to take care of them. She will never nag you about spending so much on a new Stetson and will always be the first to admit she was wrong when you've had a disagreement. She will never have a headache and will freely give you love and compassion whenever needed.

Adam asked God, "What would a woman like this cost?"

God said, "An arm and a leg."

The Texan overhearing the conversation asked, "What can I get for just a rib?"

IT CAN HAPPEN IN THE BEST OF FAMILIES

Dallas' Cattle Baron's Ball is one of that city's society highlights. One year, we were invited to sit with the honored guests at the head table. Those attending the gala affair were resplendent in their dress at this black-tie event. The young couple next to us could have been fashion plates on any magazine cover. They, undoubtedly, came from the cream of Dallas society. Just before dessert was served, the young man in his tux and ruffled shirt slipped from his chair and slid under the table, out of sight of those in attendance.

I leaned over to the lady with him and said, "You had better check on your husband, he just slid under the table."

"No!" replied the lady, "My husband just walked in the door."

TALL IN THE SADDLE

Men in Texas have the reputation of being tall and lanky, but it's not just the men who grow tall in Texas. A man in Lubbock walked into the classified department of the newspaper and asked, "How much will it cost to put an ad in the paper? I'm getting married in a few days."

"Fifty cents an inch," replied the clerk.

"That's going to be pretty expensive," replied the future groom. My fiancée is six foot two."

ON TEXAS CULTURE AND LIFESTYLES

As vast as Texas is and as diverse as its culture is, its citizens enjoy lifestyles that are about as different as snowflakes. There are peculiarities in these different lifestyles that often raise eyebrows and lend themselves to provoking laughter, even among those of that region or culture. Some of the stories of these diverse lifestyles are worth passing on. They are not told to ridicule the individuals about whom they are told, but instead to allow the reader to become better acquainted with the lifestyles of our state through laughter.

COURTESY DERAILED

The coming of the iron horse to Texas was one of the state's great progressive steps. It shrunk the vastness of the state for travelers, bringing comfort and speed to those traversing our state. While a serious business, railroading in Texas was not bereft of humor. One of my best stories was told about the state's most famous line, the Santa Fe. This giant railroad built its popularity on the friendliness and courtesy of its employees. During the years of the Great Depression, having a railroad job was considered choice employment.

The Santa Fe was known for its helpful Pullman porters and friendly conductors. A story is told that permits us to see that even these people were human and had lapses in their courteous behavior from time to time.

A lady boarded a train in the railroad hub of Temple en route to Dallas. She carried what was described by one passenger as "The ugliest baby I ever saw!" One conductor, letting his guard down, made an unkind remark about the poor ugly baby to a colleague. This was, unfortunately, overheard by the passenger. She broke down and started to cry. Seeing the sobbing passenger, a "Butcher boy," which was the name given to boys who went through the train selling candy and fruit, in an attempt to pacify the unhappy customer, went to her. "What's wrong lady," he asked.

"One of the conductors insulted me," replied the lady.

"I'm dreadfully sorry!" apologized the salesman. "Here, here, now, don't you cry," he begged the customer. "I'll report the man to his boss, I'm sure he will be punished," he assured her. The woman, still holding her baby, thanked the man for his courtesy. As he turned to walk away, the boy turned to her and said, holding out a banana, "And here's a free banana for your monkey!"

DON'T BLAME BAYLOR!

A family of reputation in Connecticut searched diligently for a school that was refined enough to send their naive, untraveled eighteen-year-old daughter to get her higher education. Someone told them about Baylor Baptist University in Waco, Texas. The school, they were told, had a great reputation for its morality and supervision, particularly in the campus dormitories where the young women stay. This was, they were assured, a fine atmosphere in which they could entrust their daughter. Knowing their daughter had received a fine upbringing, they had no doubt that under the school's supervision she would return the same demure girl they sent, but with a well-rounded education.

She was gone about a month when her mother received an unsettling letter from their darling. The letter said, "The food here in Texas is terrible, but I think I am putting on weight. If the scales in the co-ed dorm are correct, I weigh 110 pounds without my clothes."

TEXAS BLONDES LIVE UP TO REPUTATION

Blondes have, perhaps unjustly, gained the reputation of being a little dumb! The following story does little to erase this stigma. Three women escaped from the Goree unit of the Texas prison system; one was a redhead, one a brunette, and one a blonde. They made their way unnoticed to a farm just outside of Huntsville, where they hid in the loft of a barn.

When they climbed up into the loft they found three gunnysacks. They decided to put them over their heads for camouflage. About an hour later, a county sheriff and his deputy came to the barn searching for the female escapees. The sheriff told his deputy to go up in the hayloft to search for the trio.

After he came down, he was asked what he saw. The deputy told him he saw only three gunnysacks. The sheriff told him to find out what was in them. So the deputy returned to the hayloft and kicked the first sack in which the redhead was hidden, and she went, "Bow-wow." The deputy told the sheriff there was a dog in the first bag.

He then kicked the second bag in which the brunette was hidden. The brunette went, "Meow." The deputy told the sheriff the second sack held a cat.

Then, he kicked the one with the blonde in it. There was no sound at all. So he kicked it again, and the blonde said, "potatoes."

FRIENDLY TEXAS ADVICE

An implement salesman calling on a rancher in Uvalde asked the rancher, "If I run across your pasture, can I catch the five o'clock train to Dallas?"

"Certainly," replied the friendly Texan, "and if my bull happens to be in the pasture when you run across it, you can catch the four-thirty!"

DUCKS UNLIMITED
HAVE NO FEAR!

Like many men in Texas, my friend Ray Sims is an avid duck hunter. He usually has no trouble bagging the limit. But on one trip with his hunting partner, Doug, his trip to the blinds was an embarrassing flop! His aim was, to say the least, less than accurate. He had, after several cold and damp hours, brought down only a couple of ducks.

At the end of the day, as the men climbed into Ray's Suburban to start home, he said to Doug, "I am really ashamed of myself today. I think I'll go home and shoot myself!"

To this, a usually sympathetic Doug said, "Better take two bullets!"

PRIORITIES THROUGH THE EYES OF A RANCH HAND

Admittedly, this story could have taken place in any rural setting, however, it was told that it happened on a West Texas ranch. While many rural homes have no indoor plumbing, many have cesspools into which toilets, sinks, and bathtubs drain. These must be cleaned out periodically to prevent stopping up. It was told that two ranch hands were put to work cleaning out the spread's cesspool.

During the process, one worker's jacket slipped from his grasp fell into the cesspool. He left his helper to go to the house to find a pole long enough to fish out the jacket. When he returned his helper said, "I am astounded that you would consider salvaging your old jacket, considering what condition it will be in after falling into the cesspool. I've seen your old jacket and it was almost threadbare."

"I'm not worried about the jacket," replied the ranch hand. "But my lunch was in the pocket!"

CHARITY BEGINS AT HOME!

In the circuit riding days in Texas a preacher was making his circuit through West Texas when a member of a congregation he visited asked him, "Pastor, why is it you're so gaunt and thin and your horse is so sleek and fat?"

To this, the preacher replied, "I feed my horse, and my churches feed me."

BOWL OF RED, PLEASE

Jerry Alexander of Longview had the signal honor to be in Terlingua the day of one of the state's biggest chili cook-offs. He was able to purloin the notes of the three judges after all the entries had been judged. I asked his permission to share them, which he allowed me to do, after an immunity of prosecution agreement was worked out. The notes, as best I can decipher from his chili-stained Big Chief tablet, are as follows:

The first judge, whom we shall call Fred to protect the innocent, noted, "I was honored to be selected, perhaps because of my notoriety, to be a judge at this year's chili cook-off. Standing next to the judging booth when the original judge called in sick as a result of last year's judging, didn't hurt none, either. I agreed, after I was assured that none of the chili would be too spicy! And I was told I could have free beer during the judging. I accepted this job, which I looked at as a Texan's responsibility, if one was to hold one's head up. After all look what Jim Bowie did at the Alamo, and he was down with a virus, or something!"

Fred's results are as follows:

Chili #1—Mike's Maniac Monster Mobster chili

"Holy Smokes, what is this stuff? You could remove dried graffiti from the stucco wall of the hardware store with it!"

Chili #2—Arthur's Afterburner Chili

"Keep out of reach of children! I am not sure what I'm supposed to taste, besides pain." I had to wave off two people who wanted to give me the Heimlich maneuver.

Chili #3—Felix' Famous Burn Down the Barn Chili

"Call the EPA, I've located a uranium spill. My nose feels like I've been sneezing Drano!" By now the other judges know my routine and stand clear as I head to the beer line.

Chili #4—Bubba's Black Magic Chili (No doubt an East Texas entry)

I felt something scraping the taste buds off my tongue so, as a result, was unable to give it a fair taste. "Come back next year, Bubba!"

Chili #5—Linda's Legal Lip Remover

Unless it is Sunday already and the mission in Lajitas is having service, my ears are ringing. Linda seemed hurt when I told her that her chili gave me brain damage.

Chili #6—Susan's Screaming Sensation Chili

You could put a hand grenade in my mouth and pull the pin and I wouldn't notice! Back to the beer stand!

TEXANS DO WELL AT HIGHER EDUCATION

"Just to establish some parameters," said the professor to the student from Arkansas, "what's the opposite of joy?"

"Sadness," said the student.

"And the opposite of depression?" he asked the young lady from Oklahoma.

"Elation," she said.

"And you, sir," he said to the young man from Texas. "How about the opposite of woe?"

The Texan replied, "Sir, I believe that would be giddy up!"

TEXANS BEFORE THE BAR OF JUSTICE

Texans have long-since distanced themselves from the times when Judge Roy Bean's court was dealing with criminals whose usual crimes involved cattle rustling, horse theft, lead poisoning from a six-gun, and barroom brawling.

Today, the court's dockets are clogged with cases of petty theft, simple assault, and auto thefts. The following stories reveal some of the scenarios taking place in Texas courtrooms:

One man, accused of assaulting his neighbor, was asked by the judge, "Did you assault your neighbor as charged?"

"Yes," proclaimed the defendant, "I hit him with two tomatoes!"

"If," asked the judge, "you hit him with two tomatoes, how do you explain the large bump found on the back of his head by the doctor?"

"Well," answered the prisoner, unashamed, "the tomatoes were in a can!"

Another man was hauled before the court and charged with grand theft auto. "Why," asked the judge, "would you steal a car in broad daylight?"

The accused smiled, sheepishly and replied, "The car was parked by a cemetery and I assumed the owner was dead."

Some twentieth-century criminals seem to never learn! One burglar, recently released on parole met his former cellmate, who was also imprisoned for breaking and entering, on the streets of downtown Dallas. "And, asked the burglar, how are things going for you since your release?"

"Wonderful," answered the ex-con, "I opened a prosperous new business, just this week."

"And," inquired the burglar, "with what?"

"Dumb question," replied the parolee. "With my crowbar, of course!"

FACING THE FACTS

There are times when facing the facts can be painful, as this Texas ranching story vividly points out. Three boys always loved to visit their grandparents in West Texas. Not only did they love the old folks, but they loved their ranch where they could saddle up a horse at will and go for a ride on the prairie that surrounded their grandparent's ranch. Being Houston boys, the ranch experience was thrilling for the three siblings, as well as an ego booster. When they got back to Houston they made the other kid's green with envy bragging about their short, but exciting, return to the Old West!

One morning after grandma had cooked a typical ranch-style breakfast and grandpa was sitting in a rocker on the front porch, the three boys went to the aging man. "Grandpa," said the first boy, "will you make a sound like a frog?"

The grandpa, being in sort of an ill mood, said, "No, son, I don't feel like making a sound like a frog this morning."

The second boy, said, "Granddaddy, please make a sound like a frog."

To the second request, the old man said, "Boys It is really too early to play games, maybe another time I'll make a sound like a frog!"

This being their last day of their visit to the ranch, the third grandson begged, "Grandpa, we're leaving today, won't you, please make a sound like a frog?"

A little aggravated, grandpa asked the oldest of his grandsons, "Why do you all insist I make a sound like a frog?"

The little boy replied with a hopeful face, "Well, Mom said that when you croak we will get the ranch!"

STEREOTYPED TEXANS

For some reason, perhaps because Texas was such a wild frontier, Texans are often stereotyped as friendlier than most, but rather uncultured and somewhat unlearned compared with residents of other regions. The following were offered to me as someone's opinion of what, as a result of his culture, you will never hear a Texan say:

1. I'll take Shakespeare for a 1,000, Alex.
2. Duct tape won't fix that.
3. Lisa Marie was lucky to catch Michael.
4. Come to think of it, I'll take a Heineken.
5. We don't keep firearms in this house.
6. Has anybody seen the side burns trimmer?
7. You can't feed that to a dog.
8. I thought Graceland was tacky.
9. No kids in the back of the pickup; it's not safe.
10. Wrasslin's a fake.
11. We're vegetarians.
12. I'll have grapefruit instead of biscuits and gravy.
13. Honey, do these bonsai trees need waterin'?

14. Give me the small bag of pork rinds.
15. Deer heads detract from the decor.
16. Spittin' is such a nasty habit.
17. I just couldn't find a thing at Wal-Mart today!
18. Trim the fat off that steak.
19. The tires on that truck are too big.
20. I've got it all on floppy disk.
21. Unsweetened tea tastes better.
22. Would you like your fish poached or broiled?
23. Moon pies have too many fat grams.
24. She's too old to be wearin' a bikini.
25. Checkmate.
26. Does the salad bar have bean sprouts?
27. I don't have a favorite college team.
28. Be sure you bring my salad dressing on the side.
29. Those shorts ought to be a little longer, Darla Jean!
30. Elvis who?

SOME DAYS YOU
JUST CAN'T WIN!

A Texas businessman driving through the beautiful Texas Hill Country on a typically scorching summer day found himself with a flat tire on a back woodsy country road several miles from a service station. Although traveling in unfamiliar territory, he decided to remove the crippled wheel and roll it back to the last crossroads where he remembered seeing a small service station. He had rolled the lopsided wheel about a mile on the dusty chalk road, and his mouth was so dry, as the locals say, "he was spittin' cotton."

Luckily, he noticed a farmhouse not far off the road, behind which a woman was washing clothes. Knowing the local's reputation for being friendly, he decided to stop for a much-needed drink of water. The sympathetic, friendly old lady directed him to a well near the back porch of the house.

She said he could draw a bucket of cool well water and use the gourd dipper provided for drinking from the well. The dipper was a long handled dried gourd with the bowl cut open for drinking water. While unfamiliar to the traveler, these dippers are part of the rural culture in these parts.

The very thought of the cool well water on such a bone-dry day brought tears to the man's eyes! After drawing a bucket of the cool, thirst-quenching water, under the watchful eye of the very old lady, the man dipped a gourd full of the life-saving liquid. As he was about to drink, he looked at the face of his hostess.

Time had brought wrinkled lines to the mouth and chin of the living antique. Each of the crinkled wrinkles around the old lady's mouth and chin were filled with the amber juice of the snuff being dipped by the lady.

The snuff flowed in such quantity in every wrinkle that it actually dripped onto her gingham apron. Each time the traveler started to put the dipper to his lips to drink, he looked at the lips and chin of the dipper's owner. Hot and thirsty as he was, the sight of the dripping snuff dissuaded him from partaking of the cool water! Time and again he was drawn to the gourd dipper, but as it reached his lips he looked at its rim, and also at the old lady's brown-stained chin, and resisted the temptation to drink.

Then, as if a miracle, or as a result of his store-bought education, he observed that the handle of the gourd dipper was hollow. "Thank God!" he muttered, inwardly. He filled the dipper to the brim, and, putting the end of the hollow handle into his parched mouth, tilted the dipper until the cool, satisfying water flowed downward into his mouth. Seeing this, the old lady broke into convulsive laughter.

"What is so funny, inquired the traveler?"

"Aye Gad," swore the old lady, "In all my 80 years, you're the first person I've ever seen who drank from a dipper the same way I do!"

DALLAS FOLKS ARE SO SMART!

J. Frank Dobie, recognized as the dean of Texas writers, told a story that verifies that not all humor involves joke telling. His story proves that humor is found in abundance in daily life.

While he was working as a writer for the *Dallas Morning News*, his small niece arranged to visit him in the big city of Dallas. The little girl lived in a very small Texas town—one in which no colored people lived. Frank Dobie said he arranged to meet her at the bus station, and as she got off the bus a colored woman got off an incoming bus. The little girl said, "Look, Uncle Frank, that woman's face is black. And," continued the girl with a surprised voice, "her arms are black, too."

Dobie told us he looked at the naive little girl and said, "Darling, the woman is black all over!"

At this, Dobie's niece looked admiringly at her uncle and said, "Uncle Frank, you know everything!"

MUST HAVE SCOTCH BLOOD

Down in the Texas Hill Country, where German settlers' frugality still prevails, the story is told about a well-known resident in Fredericksburg who walked into a drugstore and told the druggist, "I need a bottle of aspirin."

After paying for the drug, the customer walked casually out of the store. He had barely cleared the front door when he heard the druggist calling after him. The druggist was running at a brisk trot! "Mr. Heinrich, did you order aspirin?"

"Yes, I did," said the customer. "Well, give me back the bottle," requested the druggist, as he held out his hand.

"What's wrong?" asked Mr. Heinrich.

"I'm sorry, but I gave you the wrong bottle, I gave you cyanide!"

"And what is the difference?" asked the surprised customer. Knowing his customer's frugality, the druggist answered, "Three dollars fifty cents!"

RURAL LIFE IN TEXAS MUST BE LEARNED

History shows us that traveling salesmen, or "drummers," as they were called, were often featured in Texas humor. One reason is the fact that they were often rural folks' only contact with city life. There is a story about a salesman who found himself stranded on the back roads of East Texas, due to car trouble. He approached the nearest farmhouse and inquired if he might spend the night until help could be arranged. The farmer assented, explaining to him that he would have to sleep with his small son. The salesman gladly agreed and was directed to the little boy's room. After climbing in bed with the boy, he had barely settled in when the child climbed out of bed and knelt by the side of the bed.

The embarrassed man felt somewhat guilty at the boy's piousness. Feeling that he should set a good example, he too, left the bed and knelt by his side of the bed. "What are you doing?" asked the small boy.

"The same thing you are," answered the visitor.

"Gee Whiz!" exclaimed the boy, "Mama is going to be awful mad; the pot is on this side of the bed!"

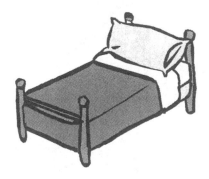

RIGHT ON BOTH COUNTS!

A man who obviously had far too many longnecks boarded a bus in Houston. Being a Saturday, the bus was overflowing with shoppers. Riders were standing in the aisle. Finally the man spotted a vacant seat by a middle-aged woman about halfway through the bus. He muscled his way toward the rear of the bus. When he got closer, he could see that this woman was, beyond doubt, one of the ugliest women he had ever encountered. Taking the seat, he tried to engage the woman in friendly conversation just to make the time pass quicker. "Don't talk to me young man. You are far too drunk to converse with," said the woman.

Offended by the woman's attitude, the man said. "And you, lady, are one of the ugliest women I've ever seen!"

"And," countered his seat partner, "you are drunk!"

Not willing to let the matter drop, the man said, "you are really ugly!"

"But," answered the woman, "you are drunk."

"I may be drunk," said the man in a voice loud enough for those around him to hear, "but tomorrow I'll be sober!"

WHAT HAPPENED TO FRONTIER COURAGE?

Not all members of the Texas Highway patrol are suitable material for today's Texas Rangers. Candidates are given extensive examinations including an oral exam by a Ranger captain. One patrolman was rejected after the following exchange during the oral examination.

Captain: "If you were by yourself in a patrol car and were pursued by a known gang of dangerous criminals in another car doing forty miles per hour, what would you do?"

The candidate looked puzzled for a second, and then replied, "Fifty!"

TEXAS FARM LIFE, A LEARNING EXPERIENCE

A South Texas farmer was milking one morning. He looked up from his milking just in time to see a fly buzz into the cow's left ear. When he returned to his milking he saw a fly swimming in the milk bucket. Just verifies the old saying, "In one ear and out the udder!"

UNDERSTANDABLE MISTAKE

A young Texas construction worker was shopping in a super market with his father when he saw a woman who was the fattest women he had ever seen. He pointed her out to his father, saying, "Ain't that the fattest woman you ever saw?"

His father, fearing the woman might overhear his son commenting on her obesity, cautioned him about his remarks. They had barely gotten down the first aisle when they ran into the fat woman again. "Just look at her, Dad," the young man said.

The father shushed his son again. "Please, son, don't say anything else about the woman's being fat. I'm afraid she will hear you!"

"Well," said the construction worker, "she should be embarrassed, as fat as she is!"

When the two men finished shopping they pushed their carts into the line at the checkout counter. Upon arrival the young man noticed they were directly behind the woman, who took up several spaces in the line. The young man's father once again cautioned his son about commenting on her size. By the time her groceries were checked and bagged, they stood only inches behind her.

Suddenly, the woman's wristwatch alarm sounded. "Beep-beep-beep" went the alarm in a high-pitched signal. The young man, being accustomed to being on a construction site, turned to his father and said, in a voice slightly louder than a whisper, "Look out, Dad, she's backing up!"

133

WHERE IS THE EMERGENCY EXIT?

A cowboy on a trail drive near Abilene sauntered into a saloon and bellied up to the bar. "What'll you have?" asked the bartender.

"I'll have ten whiskeys," replied the cowboy. With this, the barkeep set ten glasses in front of the tall, lanky cowpoke and poured ten whiskeys. The cowboy began to drink the whiskeys as fast as he could. He tossed the drinks down one after another. "I wouldn't drink those whiskeys as fast as you are drinking," admonished the concerned barkeep.

"You would if you had what I have," said the serious-faced cowboy.

"And, what do you have?" asked the sympathetic barkeep.

"Fifty cents!" answered the now well-oiled cowboy.

YOU ASKED FOR IT

The Texas Parks and Wildlife Services have done much to preserve our state's natural resources. And much of this has been accomplished through rigid enforcement by game wardens. Sometimes, as this story illustrates, common sense is bypassed by overzealous enforcement officers. A weekend get-away trip by one couple resulted in an example of a Texas game warden making himself the victim of his overzealousness.

The couple went to Lake Texoma on a fishing trip. The man announced he was taking the boat out on the lake to spend the day fishing. Hating to fish but loving to read, the wife decided to catch up on her reading uninterrupted by taking a second fishing boat and her book out on the lake.

She had anchored and just opened to where she left off when alongside pulled a boat with the game warden. "Lady, he politely said, you are in a no-fishing zone!"

"But, as you can see," replied the lady, "I'm reading and not fishing."

"But," said the eager young officer, "you have the equipment and I'm going to have to take you in!"

"You take me in," said the irate lady, "and I'll charge you with rape!"

"Ridiculous," replied the surprised game warden, "I haven't even touched you!"

"But," answered the lady, "you have the equipment!"

NOAH HADN'T BEEN TO WEST TEXAS

Seeing West Texas for the first time, a visitor asked a man in Pecos, "Does it ever rain out here?"

The man replied, "Remember reading about the time it rained forty days and forty nights?" The man said he recalled the story.

"Well," said the West Texan, "we got two inches."

A PENCHANT FOR GAMBLING

Since the days of the faro and poker tables of early Texas saloons, Texans have had a reputation as gamblers. This bent for taking a chance for personal gain is sometimes carried over into everyday life. An incident in one of Dallas' largest churches seems to bear this out!

The story is told that on one Sunday, the church was filled to overflowing. Even its balcony was full. During the pastor's "hell-fire and brimstone" sermon, a lady sitting in the balcony's front row, intent on catching every word of the preacher's discourse, leaned a little too far and fell from the balcony. She was saved from serious injury when her dress tail caught on the chandelier, which broke her fall. This, however, left the lady swinging to and fro. The pastor looked up and said, "Any man who gazes upon this unfortunate lady, will be struck blind."

One man, known to have a reputation for gambling, placed one hand over one eye and, true to form, said, "I'll chance one eye"!

YOU CAN'T TAKE IT WITH YOU!

The Scot's reputation for frugality, as well as practicality, was not left behind when many of them helped settle Texas. An example of this is the story of the death of one of Archer County's leading citizens. On his deathbed, the father of this large family, explaining to his three sons that no one knows for sure what follows beyond the grave, wanted to be prepared. He asked the three to promise that after his death each would put one hundred dollars in his coffin. On the day of the funeral the first son, as he walked past the casket, put a hundred-dollar bill in the open coffin. The second son also put a hundred-dollar bill in the casket. The third son put in a three-hundred-dollar check and took out two hundred dollars change!

OLD WEST HARD TO TAME

Some folks forget that handguns were still slung around the hips of some Texans up until the turn of the century. A story that illustrates our Wild West mentality is about a young man in Lubbock who was asked by his preacher why he hadn't seen his grandfather at church lately? "He died," replied the boy.

"Well, I saw him in town a few months ago and he looked healthy at the time, what happened to him?"

"He hit his thumb with the hammer while hanging a picture," replied the boy.

"But," retorted the minister, "that isn't enough to cause his death!"

"Yes," said the boy, "but Dad heard him yelling and thought he was having a fit and shot him."

HOME, HOME, ON THE RANGE

Two West Texas cowpokes were looking down from a mountain plateau onto the plains, which were black with a herd of buffalo that stretched as far as the eye could see. One cowboy turned to the other and said, "Do you realize that in a few short decades all these buffaloes will be gone?"

Upon hearing the comment, one old bull buffalo turned to another and said, "I thought I heard a discouraging word!"

LANGUAGE BARRIER, OR TOTAL HONESTY?

In the German-settled town of Schulenburg, a local fellow advertised a horse for sale as follows: "Two-year-old sorrel gelding 16 hands high, will sell cheap." An interested resident came by to discuss buying the horse.

"Is the horse in good health," he asked. "Yes," replied the seller.

"Then, why are you selling him so cheap?" inquired the buyer.

"The horse doesn't look good," replied the seller.

"Let me take a look at the sorrel," asked the buyer. The farmer pointed out a fine-looking sorrel tied in the corral. The tall handsome horse was a fine specimen of horseflesh, in the opinion of the buyer, who had already checked the horse's teeth.

When a price was struck, the seller told the buyer, "If the horse is found not to be as advertised, I'll refund your money." The buyer paid for the horse and left.

A week later the buyer returned leading the horse. "I want my money back," he told the seller. "The horse you sold me is blind."

"I can't refund your money," said the farmer. "I told you the horse doesn't look very good!"

TEXANS THINK BIG

Although not limited to Texas, outhouses are a standard fixture on most rural Texas residences. The story is told how a cowpoke entered an outhouse just in time to see another cowhand throw a twenty-dollar gold piece into one of the holes of the two-hole outhouse. "What are you doing throwing a twenty-dollar gold piece into the cesspool?" asked the cowpoke.

"Yesterday I lost a quarter in the cesspool. You don't expect me to go into that mess for a quarter, do you?"

GOOD IDEAS DON'T COME CHEAP!

A regular customer in a Larado saloon asked the barkeep, "How many barrels of beer do you usually sell each week?"

"About three," answered the barkeep.

"We have been friends for many years," said the customer. "Would you like an idea that would increase your weekly sales to four barrels?"

"Sure," said the barkeep, "I would be grateful for any idea that would increase my sales to four barrels!"

"Fill the glasses completely full!" said the customer.

AT LEAST IT'S IN TEXAS!

Three Texans in the hospital suffering from the same terminal illness are notified by their doctor they all have but three months to live. As part of his council of terminal patients he asks each patient how they are going to spend their last three months on earth. The first man says he is going to play golf daily for his last three months. The second man says he is going to sell all his goods and travel the world. The third man's answer was a little more puzzling to the doctor. "I'm going to move to College Station and live out my final days on earth."

"And," said the doctor, "why have you selected College Station to live out your days on earth?"

"Because," replied the third patient, "three months in College Station seems like an eternity!"

LIFE'S OLDEST PLOY BACKFIRES

Life in rural Texas isn't much different, in many respects, than it is in other parts of the country. To prove this, the following story is offered:

On a lonely, moonlit country road, as the boy's aging pickup's engine coughed and sputtered, it finally came to a total stop! As he and his date sat there, the following conversation took place: "That's funny," said the young man, "I wonder what that knocking was?"

"I can tell you one thing for sure," said his date, emphatically. "It sure wasn't opportunity!"

ADVANCE MARKET RESEARCH A MUST!

Two young Dallasites were enjoying themselves at a bungee-jumping tower set up at a local amusement park. One of the young men came from a well-to-do family. He told his friend, "I think we could make a killing setting up a bungee-jumping tower down on the Mexican border." He continued, "They have little in the way of entertainment down on the Rio Grande." Having his own financing, the first young man found little resistance from his friend, who thought it would be a great adventure as well as a good business deal.

The second young Texan said, "Let's set up in Laredo; this would give us customers on both sides of the river to draw from." They both agreed and after pooling their resources, had a tower and the other equipment shipped to Laredo. As they were constructing the tower a crowd of onlookers began to appear. The young men had arranged for everything they required, the tower, elastic cord, harnesses, insurance, etc.

Upon completion of the tower they decided to demonstrate the sport. The first young man jumped. As expected, he bounced a few times at the bottom when he reached the end of the cord. He then snapped suddenly back upward toward the jumping platform. When he reached the top, his partner noticed he had several scratches and bruises. He decided to make a second jump. Once again he bounced several times before being snapped upward toward the platform. His partner saw that one arm was hanging limp and he was nearly unconscious. He also had several severe bruises.

Realizing something was wrong, his friend asked him, "Is the cord too short?"

"No," said the first young man, "the cord is fine, but what the heck is a piñata?"

SORE LOSER

A man in Fort Worth wrestled what was obviously a heavy suitcase into a neighborhood bar he frequented. The man took a seat at his usual place at the bar and ordered a beer. As he sat there slowly sipping on his beer, the barmaid noticed what a long, sad face he had. She commented on his gloomy attitude. "You are usually so cheerful and the life of the party, why the long face?" she asked.

The man looked slowly up from his beer and replied, "I won the Texas lottery yesterday!"

"Man!" said the barmaid, "you should be jumping with joy. As a matter of fact, you should be buying for the house!"

"But," interjected the customer, "my wife washed my lottery ticket in my shirt pocket, and I can't claim my winnings."

"If that happened to me," the waitress replied, "I'd cut my spouse into little pieces."

The customer looked up solemnly and said, "What do you think I got in my suitcase?"

MISTAKEN IDENTITY

The uniqueness of Texas is accepted worldwide. Its male residents are often tagged with the nickname "Tex." This is particularly true in all branches of the military. Hardly a unit exists in any branch of the service that does not have at least one man who answers to the name "Tex." While serving on a naval ship in the 1950s, I was introduced to a sailor by the name of "Tex" Baum. As was to be expected, I asked Tex where he came from in Texas. I was surprised when he replied that he was from Shreveport, Louisiana.

"Why, then," I asked, "do they call you 'Tex'?"

"Because," he replied, "I don't want to be called 'Louise'!"

TOO MANY BUGS IN THE METRIC SYSTEM

One European, after returning from his first visit to Texas, told his neighbor, "The reason Texas will never use the metric system is they think a centimeter is something to be stepped on!"

TRANSLATORS NEEDED FOR NASA

The former state senator from El Paso, himself a Hispanic, told a gathering that the reason no Mexican-Americans were employed by NASA at Cape Canaveral, now Cape Kennedy, was because every time the director announced it was time to launch, the Hispanics all sat down to eat!

HOW 'BOUT A TEN-GALLON SAILOR HAT, SIR?

There are probably more nonswimmers in Texas than any other state with the exception of New Mexico and Arizona. The arid condition is probably the reason. But no one is more patriotic than Texans. When the Second World War started, one cowboy from the Lubbock area beat a hasty trail down to the government office to volunteer for service. When asked what branch of service he wanted to serve in, the Texan replied, "The Navy, Sir."

The recruiter asked, "Can you swim?"

"Why," asked the Texan, "haven't you got any ships?"

CONVERSATION OVER A LONGNECK

A lanky cowboy, sporting the biggest belt buckle in Travis County and showing it off in every boot-scootin' dancehall in the same area, was heard asking another jeans-clad devotee' of the country music Carnegie Halls in Texas, "What do middle-aged women and cow patties have in common?"

"Never considered the two in the same breath," replied the other dancer.

"The older they are, the easier they are to pick up!" replied the first cowboy as he parked his half-empty longneck on a table next to the wooden dance floor.

LIFE ON A TEXAS FARM

Sometimes good-humored Texans can display their humor in such a way that it stings a little.

Such is the case in a story told by a farm implement salesman calling on farmers in the region around Brownwood, Texas. He said he pulled up in front of a farm and, seeing only a young boy playing in the front yard, asked if his father was around? "Yes," replied the well-mannered boy, pointing toward the rear of the property. "He's out back at the pig pen. He won't be hard to find," the boy continued, "he's the one wearing a hat!"

YOU JUST NEVER KNOW!

The middle-aged owner of a Panhandle ranch decided that his five-year-old son was now old enough to say his own prayers at night before bedtime. That night, being new to this, under his father's supervision, he kept his prayer short and sweet! "God bless Uncle Ed," is all he said, and then kissed his father goodnight.

The very next day his Uncle Ed was run over by a bus and killed!

The family buried Uncle Ed and tried to get on with their lives. When the boy resumed his prayers, it was again a short one. "God bless grandpa," he said.

As fate would have it, grandpa dropped dead of a heart attack the next day!

The family had a funeral for grandpa and went on with their lives. When things settled down, the boy and his father resumed the boy's nightly prayers.

The boy prayed, "God bless Daddy." With recent events in mind the father was plenty scared! He was convinced he would be the next family member to die suddenly. The next morning the boy's father didn't even shave for fear of cutting his own throat. He wouldn't even ride his horse to the corral for fear of being thrown and his neck being broken. He put off his planned branding of calves in fear of a fatal burn. He even refused to play cards with his ranch hands for fear of an argument resulting in a shooting.

After walking to his house after an unusually uneventful day, which he was surprised that he survived, he was greeted by his wife. "Hi, Honey, how was your day?"

"Oh, just terrible I feel sick to my stomach."

His wife says, "You think that's bad, our poor ranch foreman was gored to death by a bull at the cattle auction today!"

DON'T GET AHEAD OF THE STORY

A foursome of ladies was playing a round of golf at one of Dallas' fashionable country clubs. One lady, despite the group's social standing, insisted on telling a ribald story at every other hole. The stories were generously sprinkled with four-letter words that would embarrass a sailor.

After several such stories the other members of the foursome said, "If you tell one more off-color story, we are going to stop playing and go home."

Several holes later, at about midmorning, the foulmouthed lady said, "I heard yesterday that at noon today the sheriff is going to pick up every known prostitute in Dallas!" With these remarks, the other ladies threw down their clubs and started toward their cars.

"Don't be in such a rush," said the offending lady, "its only ten o'clock!"

NOBODY'S PERFECT

A fellow from El Paso died one day and found himself waiting in the long line of souls awaiting judgement. Some were allowed to march right through the gates into Heaven. Others were led over to Satan, who threw them into a burning pit.

But, ever so often instead of hurling a soul into the burning pit, he tossed the poor soul off to one side in a small pile. After watching Satan do this several times the curious fellow from El Paso tapped the devil on the shoulder and said, "Excuse me, oh Prince of Darkness, but I am waiting for judgement and have to ask, why are you tossing some souls aside instead of flinging them in the pit of fire?"

"Ah," groaned Satan, "those are from Houston and are too wet to burn!"

"TAUGHT TO THE TUNE OF A HICK'RY STICK"

In the early days of rural Texas, most schooling was accomplished in small one-room schoolhouses. Discipline was as much a part of "larnin'" as readin', ritin', and 'rithmatic. And parents usually dispensed punishment in equal parts as was administered at the schoolhouse.

One mother asked her son, "Were you a good boy in school, today?" To which the boy replied, "What else could I be, standing in the corner all day?"

A FATE WORSE THAN DEATH?

Not all cases of cattle rustling were dealt with by the "law of the rope" as this story illustrates. A Winkler County man was visiting a neighbor in the local hospital, when he looked in the door of the room across the hall and saw another neighbor lying in bed with both legs in traction. After he finished visiting his friend he walked across the hall and stepped into the room of the other West Texan.

It was then he noticed the poor man not only had both legs in traction but also had plaster casts on both arms. "What on earth happened to you," he asked.

"I had a severe seenus problem," was the patient's reply.

"You mean, sinus, don't you?"

"No," the man said with a wry smile, "Me and my ranch foreman were branding a couple of my neighbor's cows that strayed on my ranch, and he seenus!"

ANOTHER REASON
COWMEN HATE SHEEP

A professor from Texas A&M University was driving through the South Plains when his way was suddenly blocked by the largest flock of sheep he had ever seen. There was a virtual sea of the wooly creatures. Seeing an opportunity to impress a lonely West Texan with his education, he stepped from his car and approached the single shepherd herding the giant flock. "If I tell you the exact number of sheep in your flock, will you give me one of your sheep?"

"Yes," answered the shepherd. "If you can tell me the exact number of sheep, you may take your pick." The professor took a few steps backward and peered out across the sea of sheep. After a few minutes, he turned to the shepherd,

"You have exactly 3,439 sheep."

"Amazing," said the shepherd, "you are exactly right. You may select any sheep you want." The professor selected an animal, tucked it securely under his arm, and turned to walk back to his car.

The shepherd called him back. "Tell me how you were able to count my sheep, please."

"I guess I took advantage of you," said the professor, "I am a university professor!"

The shepherd said, "Will you give me a chance to get even? If I can tell you where you teach, will you give me my sheep back?"

"Sounds fair to me," said the professor.

The shepherd said, "You teach at Texas A&M."

As the professor turned to return the animal he had won, he asked the shepherd, "But, how did you know where I taught?"

"Because you had my sheep dog under your arm," replied the shepherd.

SHERIFFIN' IS MORE COMMON SENSE THAN BOOK STUFF

Sheriff Tolliver, of a small South Texas county, was short a deputy and put out the word that he was interviewing for the job. Gomer Bodine wasn't the brightest guy in the county, but he was the sheriff's only candidate.

"How much is one and one?" asked the sheriff.

"11," shot back Gomer as quick as a flash.

"Can't say you are wrong on that one," responded the sheriff "And what two days of the week start with T," asked the sheriff.

Gomer studied for a brief second then said confidently, "today and tomorrow."

The sheriff glanced around the office, empty of applicants and said to the Bodine boy, "I'm going to accept that, son. Now," said the sheriff, "who killed Abraham Lincoln?"

"Dunno, atall, sheriff, sorry," said the local boy who really wanted the job.

"Well," said the patient lawman, "Why don't you go home and study on it some and if you come up with an answer, get back to me as soon as you can!"

On the way home, Gomer stopped at the billiard hall where his friends were waiting to see how he came out in the interview.

"How'd things go?" asked his friend who ran the pool hall.

"Things went fine," said Gomer. "I'm on the job one day and already working on a murder case!"

THE ALMIGHTY DOLLAR

Nearly every small Texas town has its Saturday morning "spit 'n whittle club." This is the name usually given to a regular collection of men folks who come together each Saturday morning to gossip and discuss topics of interest, while they chew their plug tobacco and whittle aimlessly on a stick of wood, hence the name. This is particularly true of those towns that have a courthouse. Usually these men can be found occupying a bench or two in front of the courthouse.

In some regions the men include swappin' pocket-knives as a part of their carefree ritual. One Saturday morning at an East Texas county seat, three regulars of this group were passing the time of day in deep conversation. A stranger walked up who fit their description of what Jesus might have dressed and looked like.

He spoke to one of the men, inquiring how he felt. The friendly citizen said he was fine except for his regular shoulder pains. The visitor reached over and touched the old-timer on the shoulder, and immediately the man felt totally well. He was overjoyed at the remission of his nagging pain.

The stranger inquired as to how the man in the middle felt. The man said that with the exception of his chronic knee rheumatism, he was in top shape. The stranger gently touched the man on his knees and legs, and he experienced instant relief! He shouted for joy at his obvious healing.

The final man was asked if he might make room on the bench for him to sit with them. To which the third man replied, "Certainly, make yourself at home, but please don't touch me, I'm drawing disability!"

BUT HE IS TRUTHFUL!

A hired hand at a ranch near Pecos was taken to task by his employer. "You work slow, you think slow, and you eat your noon meal slow. Isn't there anything you do fast?"

"Of course," replied the ranch hand, "I get tired fast!"

SIGNS OF AGING

One elderly resident of the Hill Country went to his doctor for his annual checkup. "In general," asked the doctor, "how do you feel?"

"My greatest concern," replied the longtime patient, "is I feel like I'm growing old."

"And," queried the doctor, "what makes you feel like you are growing old?"

"Lately," answered the patient, "I find myself wondering about the hereafter."

"I find it admirable," replied the doctor, "that you are concerned for your soul."

"But, you don't understand," retorted the elderly man. "I find myself going from one part of the house to another, and when I get there I wonder what I'm here after?"

BREAKING TRADITION COMES HARD

The lifestyle and culture of our Native Americans have produced some humorous stories, none of which are meant to cast an unfavorable light on these noble and proud people. One story that illustrates the early thinking of Indians comes from a West Texas reservation.

A man was driving down a road just outside a Texas Indian reservation. He saw a brave leading his horse in the direction of a nearby community, where supplies were purchased. The brave's squaw was walking behind the horse, as was the tradition of the tribe.

Noting that the couple was walking in ankle-deep snow, the white man stopped his car and said to the brave, "Chief, wouldn't it be more comfortable for your squaw if she rode the horse?"

"Yes," answered the brave, "but, squaw no have horse!"

ON BEING FRANK IN TEXAS

A Texan can generally be counted on to be frank. If you don't want to hear the truth, better not ask the question. After eating a simple lunch in a diner, a West Texan found the price well above average. Upon paying the check he asked the cashier, "What is that around your neck?"

To this the cashier replied, "It's my necklace, what did you think it was?"

The Texan in hopes of making his dissatisfaction known, replied, "I thought it might be your garter; everything else is so high here!"

AND IT WILL SURE BE BRIGHTER THAN THE RANCH HAND!

A rancher in Abilene saw one of his ranch hands sitting up on top of the barn about midnight one night. He went out to the barn and yelled up to his hand, "What are you doing sitting up on the barn so late?"

To this, the rather unintelligent ranch hand replied, "I'm trying to figure out where the sun goes when it goes down at night."

"Well," said the rancher, "just sit right there a few hours and it will finally dawn on you!"

LEARNING TO SWIM IN TEXAS

Most kids living in rural Texas, not having access to a YMCA or other organized recreational facility, learn to swim at an early age in a nearby pond, or "tank," as it is called in Texas. Some learn in a river or lake if one is close by. There's nothing like "the ol' swimmin' hole" for learning how to swim. This was not the case for one Mills County neighbor, Joe Poovey. He liked to have drowned when his pa threw him in the Colorado River in a typical "swim or drown" speed method of teaching.

Perhaps Joe would've done better if his pa had untied the sack first.

YOU CAN'T TAKE NOTHIN' FOR GRANTED!

The West Texas landscape is dotted with watering holes for livestock. We call these ponds "tanks." One sultry summer day the young attractive daughter of a rancher felt compelled to try to relieve the heat by taking a swim in one of the ranch's tanks. She rode out to one of the deepest tanks, where she disrobed and hung her clothes on the limb of a willow that grew near the tank.

She was up to her neck in the cool, refreshing, water, when one of the ranch hands, who had ridden out to check fences, spotted the pretty young lady and rode over to get a closer look. The rancher's daughter yelled at the cowpoke and in no uncertain terms told him what a cad he was for taking advantage of her inability to protect her modesty. She instructed him to ride away while she retrieved her clothes from the tree. The ranch hand continued to sit his horse without making a move away. The girl became very angry and frustrated at her predicament!

After about an hour of the standoff, she spotted a rusty old washtub sunk in the water at the edge of the tank. She eased her way over to the tub, thinking it would provide enough cover while she made a dash for her clothes.

She slowly eased the old tub out of the water, and pulled it in front of her as a shield. While holding the tub in front of her with both hands, she turned toward the ranch hand. Again she expressed in loud terms how disgusted she was at his lack of consideration. "Do you know what I think," asked the rancher's daughter. "Do you know what I think," she repeated in a loud voice.

After a brief pause, as if thinking, "Yes ma'am," said the cowpoke, "you think there's a bottom in that old tub!"

NECESSITY IS THE MOTHER OF INVENTION

Rural life in Texas resulted in some primitive conditions, which became commonplace to those living in the country. One simple example was the lack of window screens on the homes. This often meant tolerating flies in and around the family's dining room. Not considered a major discomfort, it still had to be dealt with. This condition lead to some humorous scenarios.

One such is the story of a mother who was surprised to find that her son had made his own lunch, even to straining his tea. "I'm surprised that you were able to find the tea strainer," said the boy's mother.

"I didn't," replied the young son, "I used the fly swatter." Seeing the frown on the face of his disapproving mother, the boy, in an effort to placate his angry mother, assured her, "Mother, I didn't use the new one, I used the old one."

TENDERFOOT'S GUIDE TO BEING A COWBOY AND GETTING ALONG IN THE BUNKHOUSE

1. Don't squat with your spurs on.
2. Don't interfere with something that ain't botherin' you none.
3. Timing has a lot to do with a rain dance.
4. The best way to eat crow is while it's still warm.
5. The colder it gets, the harder it is to swaller!
6. If you find yourself in a hole, the first thing to do is stop diggin'.
7. It doesn't take a genius to spot a goat in a flock of sheep.
8. Never ask a barber if you need a haircut!
9. If you think you're a person of influence, try ordering someone else's dog around.
10. Don't worry about bitin' off more than you can chew, your mouth is probably a whole lot larger than you think.
11. Always drink upstream from the herd!
12. If you're ridin' ahead of the herd, take a look back every now and then to make sure its still there with you.
13. Make sure it's a cow before you try to milk it!
14. When you give a personal lesson in meanness to a critter or a person, don't be surprised if they learn the lesson.

15. One plate of beans is dinner, two plates of beans is dangerous.
16. Letting the cat out of the bag is a whole lot easier than putting it back in.
17. Always take a look at what you're about to eat. Its not so important to know what it is, but it's crucial to know what it was!
18. Never leave a lit match in charge of the dynamite.
19. The quickest way to double your money is to fold it over and put it back into your pocket!
20. Never miss a good chance to shut up!

THERE IS A DIFFERENCE

The Terrell State Hospital for the mentally ill is located in Kaufman County, which is traversed by busy Highway 80. One unfortunate motorist found himself with a flat tire on the highway shoulder next to the hospital. His luck improved when he found his spare tire was fully aired. He removed the wheel cover of his crippled wheel, and as he removed the lug nuts, he placed them in the wheel cover so as not to lose them. In his haste, brought on by frustration, he slammed the wheel he was removing into the wheel cover, throwing the four lug nuts into the tall grass that bordered the ditch between the highway and the hospital fence.

He started to search the Johnson grass and weeds for the lug nuts required to hold the spare tire on the wheel. He was almost in a state of rage when the lug nuts could not be found.

Watching the entire episode, which was a distraction from his confinement, was a man who was a patient in the mental facility. Suddenly, the man offered, "Why don't you remove one of the nuts from the three remaining good wheels and use them temporarily to get to some assistance?"

Astounded, and somewhat embarrassed that he hadn't thought of the logical idea, the motorist thanked the patient and asked, "What are you doing in a mental hospital?"

The man replied, "Heck man, I may be crazy, but I ain't stupid!"

TOMBSTONE HUMOR

Although Texans take death as seriously as other folks, their humor sometimes shines through the tears, as in the case of the epitaphs on these two tombstones in cemeteries in Pecos County and in the Big Bend.

A Butterfield Stage line agent slept under the following words, which told much about his sudden demise:

"Here lies Lester Moore
Four slugs from a .44
No Les, no More."

Another testimony to the violence of the Old West was recorded on a tombstone in the Boot Hill Cemetery not far from Terlingua, Texas.

"Here lies Butch, we planted him raw.
He was quick on the trigger,
but slow on the draw."

These two examples of "tombstone humor" speak volumes about the wilder side of early Texas culture.

RED-EYE FOR TWO, PLEASE

A cowpoke stumbles into a saloon in Pecos and staggers over to the saloon's only customer at the bar.

"Can I buy you a drink?" he asks the patron.

"Sure," answers the surprised customer, "Why not?"

The cowpoke asks the man, "Where are you from?"

"I'm from San Antonio," says the patron.

"Why, I'm from San Antonio, too!" replies the cowpoke. "Let's have another drink for ol' San Antone." The patron and his newfound friend tosses down another one.

"And," asks the cowpoke, "where did you go to school?"

The patron replies, "I went to St. Mary's Catholic school on San Pedro St."

"You ain't going to believe this but I went to St. Mary's myself. Let's have a drink for good ol' St. Mary's!"

About this time one of the regulars comes in and bellies up to the bar. "What's going on?" he asks the bartender.

"Nothing much," replied the bartender. "The Simpson twins are drunk, again!"

NO SECRETS

While small towns have their charm, most, even in Texas, have certain drawbacks. For instance, in small towns everybody seems to know everybody's business. This is best illustrated by a story we were told about an incident in Kaufman, Texas.

A salesman in the Sears store pointed out to a customer that the store had a special offer on vacuum cleaners that made buying now very attractive. "If you buy a vacuum cleaner today, you won't make a payment for three months," he said.

"Have you been talking to our neighbor?" asked the customer.

RURAL TEXAS EDUCATION

Folks living in rural Texas have a language all their own. One moving to the country needs to have a few lessons in rural jargon in order to feel right at home. One example is pointed out in the following question: "What is the difference in a critter and a varmint?" A critter is what you see squashed on a Texas highway and varmint is what you do after you see it!

NOT ALL AGGIES
COME FROM A&M

The following dialog was overheard in a Ft. Worth hospital emergency room: "Nurse, ask that TCU accident victim his name, so we can notify his parents."

The nurse said to the injured young man, "Tell me your name so we can notify your parents."

"They already know my name," replied the student.

BE CAREFUL WHO
YOU TAKE UP WITH

My late brother-in-law, Jimmy Alexander, told me about the fellow who fell in love with a girl who lived in Waxahachie. About the time he learned to spell Waxahachie, she up and moved to Nacogdoches.

TOTAL MISUNDERSTANDING

On a trail drive in Pecos County one outfit came across a terrible discovery as they attempted to cross the Pecos River. The crossing point they had chosen was choked with the carcasses of forty or so steers from an earlier cattle drive.

The animals were bloated and had obviously been in the water for several days. One cowpoke sought out a spot on the river upstream from the putrefied remains of the rotting cattle to get himself a drink of cool river water.

When he found a place a safe distance away, he dipped his hat into the Pecos and filled it with the cool water. He then drank until he was filled. Which, after being on the trail for days, was most refreshing!

Another cowboy came up and watched as his friend emptied hat after hat of the refreshing water. The second cowpoke then pulled back the branches of a tree limb that dipped into the river. He pointed to the carcass of a rotting, maggot-filled steer that lay half in the river and half on the bank. The dead animal had been hidden from sight by the drooping branch! The man who had been drinking abruptly threw down his hat, jumped to his feet, and took off in a dead run up the river.

He would stop every few yards and turn to look back, obviously measuring how far he had run. He would then turn and continue running for several yards and then turn to see how far he had run. The second cowboy jumped on his horse and rode until he caught up with him. "Why are you running like a fool?" he asked him.

"My papa always said that running water purifies itself every fifty yards," was his reply.

LAW-ABIDING COWPOKE

A cowboy in Fort Stockton goes in a saloon and orders "A whiskey for my horse."

"And what for you?" asks the barkeep.

"Nothing," answers the cowpoke, "I am riding."

MAKES CENTS TO ME

The story proves that not all Texans are businessmen like Jesse Jones, Amon Carter, Ross Perot, or Clint Murchison. Two farmers sat on the "spit and whittle" bench in front of the Hood County courthouse talking agribusiness one Saturday. "I sure dread my trip to market Monday to sell my hogs," said one of the farmers.

"And why?" inquired his friend.

"Its that long drive to Kansas City," observed the first man.

"I always thought you sold your hogs in Fort Worth," said his friend.

"I usually do," replied the farmer, "but I read in the paper that hogs are bringing thirty-seven and a half cents in Fort Worth. I can make an extra quarter cent a pound if I take them to Kansas City," observed the first man.

"But," inquired the second farmer, "what about the time?"

"What's time to a hog?" answered the first farmer.

RAZOR-SHARP HUMOR

Another example of Texas humor with a bite involves a customer getting a shave in a San Antonio barbershop. The customer had only one arm. During the shave, the young barber, fresh out of barber school, had cut the customer several times. The man's face was dotted with small bits of tissue used to stop the bleeding from the numerous nicks. The young barber asked, "I'm new here and don't know the regular customers yet, do you frequent our shop often?"

"No," replied the man in the chair, "I lost my arm fighting with Sam Houston at San Jacinto."

SPACE AGE HUMOR

Houston folks grew up in the space age and regardless of their station in life, they are in tune with space technology. There is a story in Houston about a homeless man who took shelter at the base of the San Jacinto monument, which is the tallest column monument in the world. It is just a stone's throw from NASA, the home of the U.S. space activity.

After spending the night out in the cold damp air, the derelict gathered an armload of wood from the nearby brush to be used in building a fire to brew some nice hot coffee. He built the fire out of the wind at the base of the towering monument. Two passing drunks saw the blaze, and one remarked to another, "They'll never get liftoff with a puny ignition like that!"

THE BUM STEER

As much a part of the Texas psyche as the ten-gallon hat or cowboy boots is the need for Texas men-folks, as they are called, to boast of their masculinity. Perhaps that is why they have borrowed the word "macho" from their peripheral Mexican heritage to describe their manliness.

This penchant for strutting around like a gamecock has not escaped being caricatured in Texas humor. An example is a story about a Texas rancher who spent a large amount of money on a registered prize bull, with which he hoped to strengthen his herd. The rancher became frustrated when he noticed the bull seemed to take no interest in his cows. He took the bull to the local veterinarian, who pronounced the animal sound but prescribed some pills to increase the bull's potency.

The rancher took the bull back to the ranch, where he noticed, after giving the animal the pills, a marked improvement in his performance. The proud rancher could hardly wait to tell his neighbor of the miraculous recovery of the prize bull. The neighbor responded, "Wonder what those pills were?"

"Don't know," answered the rancher, "but they tasted like peppermint."

YOU CAN'T BELIEVE ALL YOU HEAR!

It is surprising how quickly Europe's favorite sport, soccer, has become popular in America. And its popularity is not limited to the big cities as evidenced by this story from the Texas Panhandle.

A few years ago, when soccer's World Cup championship games were being played, one cowboy who worked on a spread on the Canadian River surprised the manager of the local Ford house when he rode his favorite mount in and asked if they could put a light on his saddle. "Sure," said the manager, who had worked on the cowpoke's old pickup, "but why do you, after all these years, need a light on your saddle?"

The cowboy, who had become quite a soccer fan explained that he was really enjoying the World Cup series and he missed seeing the games when he had to ride the range. "But," he said, "I heard on the TV that I could pick up the games if I had a saddle light."

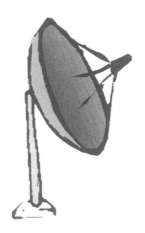

YOUTHFUL ONE-UPMANSHIP

Parker County is accepted by most Texans as the watermelon capital of Texas. One farmer near Weatherford had an exceptionally good crop one year, and one of his larger patches bordered on the sandy lane that led to the local high school. In the sultry summer afternoons it was almost expected that some of the big, overgrown boys would squeeze through the barbed wires of the fence surrounding the watermelon patch and steal a melon or two for a refreshing end to a scorching school day. The farmer didn't begrudge these forays into his watermelon patch; however, one day while mending the fence, he noticed that the students had busted several of his melons, eating only the cool, sweet, hearts of the melons, and left the rest to rot in the field.

The farmer couldn't afford this wanton waste of his largest cash crop. He had to take measures to stop the intruders. He knew the parents of all the boys and didn't want to fracture his relationship by being too harsh. He put a sign in the field which read, "Boys, I have poisoned ten of these melons!"

The next day upon inspection, the farmer, in hopes of finding results, found a crudely lettered sign which read, "Farmer, we have poisoned twenty of these melons!"

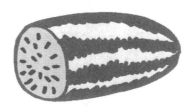

LIGHTNING STRIKES TWICE

I include this A&M story only because it was told to me by a highly respected source, who, incidentally, says he was once abducted by a spaceship. I hesitated to use it in a humor book because of its sadness. I must admit it made me bawl when I heard it.

My friend told me about an Aggie with whom he works, who got a phone call one day. After listening for a few minutes he broke into uncontrollable sobs. "Oh no, oh no!" cried the Aggie. Still in tears, he hung up the phone. His boss inquired what the distress was. The tearful young man still sobbing replied, "My mother just died."

"I am so sorry," said his boss, "would you like to go home?"

"No," replied the Aggie, "I can't help there, I'll finish out the day."

After returning to work, the man was paged for another call. He spoke for a few minutes and then, once again, broke into sobs. This time worse than before, "No, no, no!" he cried into the phone. "Not you too!" he sobbed, his shoulders shaking. Again his boss asked what the problem was. "That was my brother; his mother died too!"

HONESTY BEST POLICY?

One of my favorite stories which illustrates how Texas humor permeates every strata of Texas culture was told to me by my traveling salesman friend, Ray Sims. Ray related how, after leaving home early to eat breakfast, he stopped at one of those Hopkins County roadside diners. He was greeted by a slightly older than teenage waitress who asked, "What may I do for you?"

Ray told her, "I would like some biscuits and gravy, scrambled eggs, a nice smile, and a few kind words." In a reasonable amount of time the young lady reappeared. With a nice smile she served the food he ordered.

She then asked, "Will there be anything else?"

Ray asked her, "What about them few kind words?"

To this, the waitress leaned in close and guardedly said, "Don't eat them eggs!"

PURE NATIVE LOGIC

I am indebted to my nephew, Jerry Alexander, of Longview, for this story, which illustrates the logic we sometimes use and the conclusions we draw.

Some folks visiting Texas for the first time are disappointed because they don't see Indians on every corner. While this facet of the Old West has been tamed, Texas still has an abundance of Native Americans. Now these proud people are collected on one of several reservations.

A story is told of a young brave on one of the half dozen reservations, who had the habit of going to the nearest town each Saturday for supplies. He rode his favorite horse to the highway a few miles away from the reservation. At the highway he tied his horse and hitchhiked to town.

After shopping for supplies, he hitchhiked back to his horse. One particular weekend, after buying his supplies, the brave started his return trip and was picked up by a man in a brand new automobile. The Indian watched as the speedometer gradually crept higher and higher. When the speedometer showed 86 miles an hour, the brave remarked to the driver, "Car him overheat."

"No," said the driver, "you don't understand. The faster you go, the colder it gets."

The Indian found this revelation an astounding one. "The faster it goes, the colder it gets! Faster it goes, colder it gets," he repeated over and over in his mind all the way to where the horse was tied up.

181

Upon arrival, he untied his horse and started his ride back to the reservation. The Indian started his ride at a smooth, slow gallop. Remembering what he had learned, he thought, "The faster it goes, the colder it gets." With this in mind, despite the searing Texas heat, he began to whip his horse into a full gallop.

The faster the horse ran, the more the rider whipped him. Sooner than usual, the Indian arrived at the reservation. By this time the horse was covered in a lather of sweat! The Indian went into his teepee. Shortly, the brave heard a dull thud!

Going outside, the Indian found his horse dead as the proverbial doornail. The Indian said, "Ugggh, horse, him freeze to death!"

CELEBRITY STATUS

While many Texans have made a name for themselves in the field of country and western entertainment, their gold records do not make them totally immune from ego deflation. The story is told of one famous recording star who was scheduled to entertain in a nursing home in Fort Worth. Upon arrival he found the lobby lined with elderly men and women. Not one person acknowledged the well-known star. No autograph was requested, not even a smile was offered.

The entertainer could no longer stand the ignoring public. He walked over to a silver-haired lady and asked, "Do you know who I am?"

"No!" replied the little old lady, "but if you go to the front desk, perhaps they can help you!"

SOPHISTICATION IN EAST TEXAS

It is generally conceded that East Texas folks are considered to be honest, hard working, salt-of-the-earth folks. Although educated and certainly not backwards, they are as a rule, unsophisticated and somewhat separated from the mainstream of society. The following story is an example of their honest lack of sophistication:

My friend Bill Trobridge operates a small but successful lumber mill in the piney woods just outside of Lufkin. He recently received an official-looking typically bureaucratic letter from the Labor Department in Washington D.C. The letter simply stated "Please send us a list of all your employees (broken down by sex).

My friend shot off the following letter in reply:

Gentlemen,

I am unable to comply with your letter requesting a list of my employees broken down by sex. My employees ain't broken down by sex, they is broken down mostly by alkyhol!

Most sincerely,

Bill Trobridge

OPPORTUNITY ON EVERY CORNER

Houston is a city known far and wide as a city of unlimited opportunities. If this story is true, it carries these attributes too far. It was reported that a church in one of the city's suburbs had a display board in front on which the Sunday sermon is posted. One particular Sunday, the pastor posted his sermon as follows: "If you're through sinning, come on in!" Under the posted sermon, someone had placed a hand-lettered sign which read, "If not, call Ruby at 321-0282."

More humor and trivia from Republic of Texas Press

1-55622-648-9 · $15.95

1-55622-730-2 · $16.95

1-55622-653-5 · $17.95

1-55622-572-5 · $15.95

1-55622-526-1 · $12.95

1-55622-699-3 · $14.95

1-55622-257-2 · $12.95

1-55622-616-0 · $14.95

1-55622-683-7 · $16.95